SAFARI
IN STYLE
SOUTH AFRICA

SAFARI IN STYLE
SOUTH AFRICA

Jeremy Jowell • Ian Johnson • Martin Harvey
David Rogers • Daryl Balfour

AFRICA
Geographic

contents

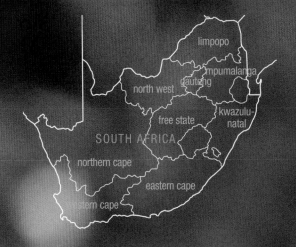

AFRICA GEOGRAPHIC TRAVEL

Taking Africa to the world.
Bringing the world to Africa.

At Africa Geographic Travel we love what we do and pride ourselves in providing a unique and intimate window on South Africa's spectacular landscapes, wildlife and cultural heritage. For more than 15 years we have been showing our readers and travellers from around the world the wonders of the African continent – in our magazines, books, expeditions and independent itineraries. At any given moment, we have guides, writers, photographers, researchers and conservationists in the field, researching and experiencing the wild and beautiful places to bring them to you.

We will show you how to get under Africa's skin, how to witness all the wildlife action and how to tread lightly so that others, too, may enjoy this magical continent. Let us help you plan your trip – all you have to do is decide when, where and how you would like to travel – and leave the rest to us.

Africa Geographic Travel
Devonshire Court
20 Devonshire Road
Wynberg 7800
Cape Town, South Africa
Tel. (+27-21) 762 2180
Fax (+27-21) 762 2246
E-mail *travel@africageographic.com*
Website *www.africageographictravel.com*

IAN JOHNSON

Menu
Sirloin with baby potato ragout & pepper sauce

Grilled line fish served with an Asian stir fry

Wild mushroom and blue cheese pasta

JEREMY JOWELL

IAN JOHNSON

DAVID ROGERS

introducing
south africa

The country that lies on the southern tip of Africa is a tapestry of fascinating contrasts. Here you'll find desert and subtropical rainforests, soaring
mountain peaks and deep, labyrinthine caves, the largest mammals on earth
and minuscule, multi-hued insects, sophisticated cities and wide, uninterrupted
horizons. Combine these factors with the 47-million-strong population, whose
cultures, beliefs and politics are as diverse as the landscape, and you have a
vibrant, electric country that has greeted the 21st century with open arms,
welcoming also the ever-increasing number of visitors who come to see South
Africa for themselves.

For many people, it's the continent's wildlife that is the irresistible magnet.
And South Africa is in the forefront of wildlife conservation, with some
1 000 national parks and private game reserves spread across the subcontinent.
The country is known as a Big Five destination. However, its other creatures,
including African wild dogs, giraffes, hyaenas, cheetahs and a host of antelope
and bird species, are no less intriguing.

This beautiful book, *Safari in Style – South Africa*, explores some of these
wildlife destinations. The travel experts at Africa Geographic, in collaboration
with our experienced journalists and photographers, have put together a selection of lodges and retreats that will send you hunting for your suitcases. We
visit the magical Western Cape, with its craggy mountains, magnificent wine
farms, moody oceans and wonderful vacation destinations. The Eastern Cape,
once fraught with frontier wars, is now popular for its elephant reserves and
tranquil beach getaways. KwaZulu-Natal offers historic hotels, coastal lodges
and other exotic retreats. We explore the great escarpment, which drops gently
as we venture further west to the more arid interior. Here are a plethora of rambling game lodges. Then there's the lowveld, home to the world-famous Kruger
National Park and the host of game-rich reserves that line its western border.

Some of the accommodation options we feature provide pampered luxury,
and offer everything the sophisticated visitor desires. Others are more homely,
without stinting on discreet service and professionalism. Others still are situated
in wilder reserve areas, where the number of visitors is limited to ensure privacy
and a low-impact footprint on the environment. The choice is yours.

Hopefully, this evocatively written and photographed *Safari in Style – South
Africa* will encourage you to pack your bags and experience for yourself the
country's finest getaways.

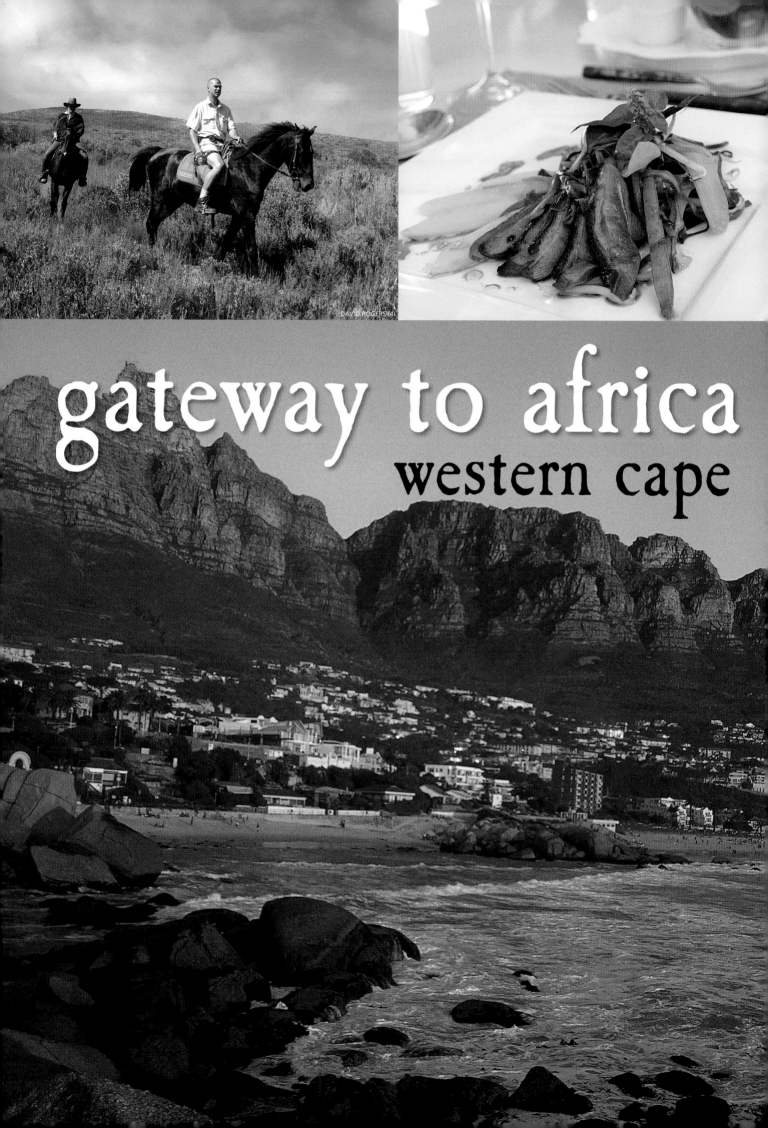

gateway to africa
western cape

JEREMY JOWELL

Camps Bay beach and the
Twelve Apostles mountain range.

The Western Cape covers the southernmost tip of Africa, and has been blessed with beautiful mountains, oceans coloured in all shades of blue, and well-watered lands for farming. Its capital, Cape Town, has world-class attractions, and its vineyards offer award-winning vintages. Add to this a plant diversity that incorporates some 9 000 species in the Cape Floral Kingdom alone, and it becomes easy to see why the Western Cape is one of South Africa's premier tourist destinations.

cape grace

Table Mountain is the famous backdrop to this elegant hotel that rises serenely above Cape Town's busy V&A Waterfront.

PREVIOUS SPREAD Cape Grace has become a landmark in Cape Town's bustling V&A Waterfront.

THIS SPREAD Whiskies galore at the Bascule Bar.

Luxury boats roll and creak gently at their moorings beneath the city's iconic mountain.

The suites offer style, comfort and grand views.

At onewaterfront restaurant, the lighting is subtle, the service discreet and the food excellent.

The hotel's heated pool.

Outside, I sit on the wharf and enjoy the view of the marina and the million-dollar pleasure boats

CAPE GRACE

Walking through Cape Grace's elegant entrance, I am pleasantly surprised when the doorman addresses me by name. In a large hotel this is a remarkable feat – and the only other place where I can recall similar courtesy is the Cape Grace's older 'sister', the Mount Grace, in the Magaliesberg. The Brand family, who started both hotels, maintained that 'people should feel that they are staying with a good friend when they visit a hotel'. The new owners, Kingdom Meikles Africa, a company that also has five-star hotels in Harare and Victoria Falls in Zimbabwe, are building on the Cape Grace legacy, and I am not surprised to learn that, in 2007, readers of the UK *Condé Nast Traveller* gave the hotel 98.57 per cent for service and staff, the highest awarded to any hotel in the world.

Cape Grace is situated in the heart of Cape Town's popular Victoria & Alfred Waterfront area, with Table Mountain at its back and wonderful views in all directions. The accommodation is classically understated, and the rooms are very elegant. All have separate bathrooms and dressing rooms, and every mod con that you would expect in a hotel of this stature. The rooms have been re-fashioned by designer Kathi Weixelbaumer, who has turned to the Cape's flora, history and geography for her inspiration. The fabrics were hand-painted by Cape Town-based African Sketchbook Fine Art Fabrics, an organisation that employs artists from local communities.

I emerge from the foyer and walk along the dock, past fishing boats preparing to head out to sea. Seagulls bob on the clear, still water, and South African fur seals plunge and surface to poke their noses above the water.

The Victoria and Alfred harbour basins, which were developed in the 1860s to handle the increased trade incurred by the gold- and diamond-mining boom in South Africa, have been thoroughly transformed over two decades into one of South Africa's top 10 tourist attractions. Today, a modern marina, excellent aquarium, more than 400 shops, dozens of restaurants and interesting historical buildings attract millions of visitors each year. One of the attractions is the Robben Island Gateway, the departure point to the island on which Nelson Mandela was imprisoned for more than two decades.

The Mother City's beautiful mountain is in glorious afternoon light as I return to the hotel for a sundowner at the Bascule Whisky, Wine and Cocktail Bar. The whisky collection, housed in the underground cellar, includes varieties found nowhere else in the world. Outside, I sit on the wharf, sipping my drink, and enjoy the view of the marina and the million-dollar pleasure boats that roll gently in the water. Another wonderful place for teas and drinks is the library, a tranquil retreat with wooden cabinets filled with books and comfortable chairs.

Later, I dine at Cape Grace's onewaterfront restaurant. Roast impala is my main dish and I ask the sommelier for a shiraz. Instead of presenting me with a wine list, she emerges with a selection of vintages in four glasses on a tray, and asks me to taste them all and make my choice. The evening ends with a sparkling dessert wine and a cheese trolley groaning beneath the weight of 40 different varieties!

After all that eating, you'll be pleased to know that the hotel has a superb spa, as well as a heated outdoor swimming pool. And, as reflected in the simple philosophy of the original owners, it is not only the doorman, but the sommelier, the waiters and the cleaners who made me feel thoroughly at home.

details

When to go
The hotel is open all year.

How to get there
Located on the city's Atlantic coastline, the hotel is just 30 minutes by road from Cape Town International Airport.

Who to contact
Tel. (+27-21) 410 7100,
e-mail *reservations@capegrace.com*
or go to *www.capegrace.com*

steenberg
hotel

There are 350-year-old buildings, fragrant gardens,

a world-renowned golf course and five-star living at

this tranquil hotel in the Constantia valley.

Steenberg has a 325-year-old history, which makes it the oldest farm in Cape Town's lush suburb of Constantia. And its 1740 manor house, the Jonkershuis ('young man's house') and other buildings, which were declared national monuments in 1969, have been caringly transformed into a luxurious five-star hotel. Here, beneath the Constantiaberg mountains, with views towards Table Mountain and just kilometres away from most of the city's major attractions, the best of the old has been lovingly harmonised with the finest of the new.

General manager Gaby Gramm believes that discerning travellers are looking for a holiday venue that makes them feel at home. 'That's why we have just 24 suites,' she tells me. The Heritage Suites are almost house-sized. Each has a master bedroom, large lounge and dining areas, a private swimming pool and magnificent views of the vineyard, golf course and False Bay. The décor blends well-turned antiques with sophisticated technology – in the Cape Colonial Suite, I would never have guessed that the large mirror is actually a television set! The décor in the Manor House recalls 17th-century life in the Cape, while the premier rooms are more modern, with open-plan bathrooms and free-standing baths.

The buildings are linked by paths that wind through formal gardens and sculpted avenues of lavender. It is here that many of the flowers for the bedrooms and the herbs and spices for the restaurant are grown. I sit on a bench and breathe in the fragrance, and listen to the sound of silence. This is a good place to relax – there's also a swimming pool, and a spa that offers a variety of therapeutic massage and touch treatments.

The buildings are linked by paths that wind through formal gardens and sculpted avenues of lavender

PREVIOUS SPREAD Flowers from the garden are used to decorate the rooms.

The old Cape Dutch buildings rise above the vivid vineyards.

THIS SPREAD Steenberg is known for its fine white wines.

The farm has stood beneath the Constantiaberg mountains for 350 years.

A shady spot and an inviting pool.

The suites are tastefully furnished with antiques and well-chosen modern pieces.

Steenberg Hotel offers discreet, personalised service.

Catharina's Restaurant has shady tables set under the oak trees and a more formal indoor dining area where, on Sundays, strains of live music float through the air. The restaurant is named for Catharina Ustings, the original owner of the farm, who arrived from Germany in 1662 and was granted a lease in 1682. I dine on steamed west coast mussels, duck breast served with a corn and chilli pancake and smooth parsnips, and a sublimely rich chocolate dessert. All were prepared under the eye of the acclaimed executive chef, Garth Almazan, and are accompanied by delicious Steenberg wines. I toast Catharina, so far from her home on the Baltic coast, and rise from the table a contented man.

Later, the farm was sold to Frederick Rossouw, and some of the buildings date back to his ownership. It was Frederick who built the historical U-shaped manor house and also made the first wines. His son Nicolaas later crowned the historic building with its fine 'holbol' gable, which is now the only remaining example of its kind. The farm was sold to the Louw family in 1842 and they farmed here until the 1990s.

Developed into a five-star hotel and golf course estate by Johannesburg Consolidated Investments, Steenberg was, in May 2005, absorbed into the stable of Graham Beck, the renowned owner of several famous vineyards. The Becks are also great lovers of art and they have contributed a large collection of bold sculptures by Edoardo Villa, which have been strategically placed round the gardens.

Steenberg is especially known for its white wines and, in 2007, in her first year as winemaker, Ruth Penfold was awarded the Diner's Club Young Winemaker of the Year Award for her Semillon.

I can think of no better place to absorb the history of this emerald valley and early life at the Cape. And I'm not the only one who enjoys the charms of this fine estate. Its magnificent 18-hole golf course, one of the city's finest, attracts visitors from around the world.

details

When to go
Steenberg Hotel is open all year.

How to get there
The hotel is a 30-minute drive from Cape Town International Airport.

Who to contact
Tel. (+27-21) 713 2222,
e-mail *info@steenberghotel.com*
or go to *www.steenberghotel.com*

winchester
mansions hotel

Guests return time and again to this gracious, palm-fronted

landmark on Cape Town's sparkling Atlantic coastline.

Don't miss the Sunday jazz brunches. They're a big hit with both locals and international visitors

Sex-on-the-Beach is particularly enjoyable, especially at sunset on Cape Town's Atlantic coast. With a satisfied smile, I sit back and languidly sip my cocktail on the terrace of the Winchester Mansions Hotel. Across the road, joggers and walkers exercise in the golden light shining on the Sea Point promenade.

After another cocktail or three, we stroll into Harvey's Restaurant, one of Cape Town's top eating establishments. The sky outside darkens and we dine by candlelight. My starter is a creamy soup of butternut and sweet potato, while my companion savours every mouthful of her lemongrass and coconut-infused quail, served on Asian-style melon salad.

My main course is grilled kingklip with couscous, peppadew, citrus risotto and fluffy mash. Dessert is a superb hazelnut and dark chocolate terrine. Back in the luxury of my suite, sleep comes easily.

Centrally located on Sea Point beachfront, close to the popular V&A Waterfront and within easy reach of the city's best beaches, Winchester Mansions Hotel is an institution in Cape Town. It has won numerous awards in the hotel and tourism industry, and was recently ranked as one of the world's best-value hotels by a leading US travel magazine.

The Cape Dutch style hotel was built in the 1920s and has an old-world elegance and grace. 'We pride ourselves in exceeding our guests' expectations,' says managing director Nils Heckscher. 'We have the infrastructure and amenities of a large hotel, but also the intimacy and personalised attention of a luxury guest-house. Many of our visitors are repeat guests who describe us as a 'home-away-from-home' hotel. And when they arrive they always get a hug from me.'

There are 51 luxurious rooms and 25 stylish suites, offering either ocean or mountain views. Top of the range is the sea-facing presidential Harvey Suite, with two double en-suite bedrooms, a lounge, dining room and kitchenette. Plans for an additional 40-suite development are also under way. The hotel welcomes children of all ages and conference facilities are also available.

The location of Harvey's Restaurant, combined with its traditional Cape cuisine and fine service, ensure an evening to remember. Dinner is often served in the colonnaded courtyard, reminiscent of an Italian piazza and encircled by palm trees and fountains.

If you time your stay to include a weekend, don't miss the Sunday jazz brunches. They're a big hit with both locals and international visitors. Winchester Mansions also hosts a monthly Grapes, Gourmet and Gallery evening, where visitors can wine and dine and enjoy an art exhibition.

Guests can pamper themselves at the Ginkgo Health and Wellness Spa, which offers a wide range of treatments, each beginning with a footbath and ending with herbal tea served in the spa's tranquillity lounge. I head there for a neck and back massage and, as the masseuse's healing hands soothe away my city stress, I drift off into a relaxed sleep.

The next morning, I wake before dawn and head out for one of Cape Town's best hikes – a short but strenuous two-hour round trip to the summit of Lion's Head.

From the starting point on Signal Hill, I ascend the path in a clockwise direction around the mountain, with views over the Atlantic seaboard unfolding beneath me. The sun rises, bathing the harbour and city in a soft light. After conquering a set of ladders and chains, I sweat out the last steep stretch to the summit where I gaze across Table Bay to Robben Island and beyond.

But breakfast is beckoning, so I hurry down the mountain to the Winchester's warm and welcoming dining room.

PREVIOUS SPREAD Set in a stunning location, Winchester Mansions Hotel is one of Cape Town's best-known landmarks.

THIS SPREAD Romantic dining in the elegant courtyard.

Fresh flowers and immaculate linen await in the bedrooms.

The food is delicious and beautifully presented.

The leafy courtyard is a tranquil retreat from the busy streets beyond the hotel's walls.

The sitting room's décor is warm and welcoming.

WINCHESTER MANSIONS

details

When to go
Cape Town is a year-round destination. The peak tourist season is mid-December to the end of March, when the hotel runs at high occupancy. It is advisable to book well in advance for this period. The best time to see flowers and whales in the Western Cape is between August and November.

How to get there
The hotel is centrally located on the Sea Point beachfront. From Cape Town International Airport, drive along the N2 to the city and take the M6 to Sea Point. The physical address is 221 Beach Road.

Who to contact
Tel. (+27-21) 434 2351,
e-mail *sales@winchester.co.za*
or go to *www.winchester.co.za*

la residence

Nestling on 12 hectares beneath the serene mountains of Franschhoek is a private hotel so luxuriously appointed that guests refer to it as a work of art.

The furniture is an eclectic mix of antiques and valuables, with Persian rugs and a fine-art collection sourced mostly from local artists

PREVIOUS SPREAD Tiled floors, comfortable ruby-upholstered chairs and sparkling chandeliers welcome guests at La Residence.

The view across thriving vineyards to the Franschhoek mountains.

THIS SPREAD Fine dining, La Residence style.

The suites, with their inviting beds and wonderful works of art, are ideal for honeymooners or lovers of romance.

Sundowners and a beautiful vista.

Furniture and artefacts from around the world have been specially selected to create Liz Biden's distinctively elegant style.

An elegant corner for a cup of fragrant coffee.

'**Our aim is to provide a home away from home** … for those who have a very privileged lifestyle,' explains Edward Morton as he leads me into La Residence in Franschhoek. We pass along a long entrance hall with palace-high ceilings and six chandeliers bristling with glass and reflecting sparkling prisms of light. Beyond lies a courtyard, where rows of palms frame the mountains. The furniture is an eclectic mix of antiques and valuables, with Persian rugs and a fine-art collection sourced mostly from local artists.

La Residence is part of the Royal Portfolio and owners Liz and Phil Biden are certainly familiar with the homes of the privileged. In 2000 they opened luxurious Royal Malewane on the border of the Kruger National Park. One year later, they launched the original La Residence and Birkenhead House in Hermanus. All were previously Biden holiday homes, and Liz's motivation for opening them to the public stemmed from her pleasure in watching others enjoy the places she'd created.

Franschhoek is a delightful small town with South Africa's highest concentration of award-winning restaurants and, around it, some of the best vineyards in the country. The name means 'French corner' and it was here that the French Huguenots settled in 1688 when escaping religious persecution in their home country. The new arrivals were skilled wine-makers. Today, there are 40 different wine cellars in the area. You can also try French cheeses at La Fromagerie, watch sabrage at Cabrière estates and get decadent at Huguenot chocolatiers.

Despite these attractions, there are very compelling reasons not to set a foot outside La Residence. Edward is an impeccable host, and the same is true for chef Chris Smit. My soya marinade duck with fresh mango and an Asian salad could easily hold up with the best in Franschhoek. 'Liz phones almost every night to make sure that everyone enjoyed the day,' Edward tells me.

I was certainly happy. I could have spent hours admiring the La Residence artworks, the fine furniture and the valuables that have been collected by Liz on her travels. There are 11 suites, each entirely different from the rest. Mine was the opulent, black-and-white Armanis suite. I also visited the Tibet room and the French suite, with its soft silks and fine linen.

La Residence, which opened in 2007, has already begun harvesting awards as one of the sexiest places to stay in the Cape winelands. But the dream for Liz Biden and her team on this 12-hectare property has only just begun. Shiraz and Cabernet Sauvignon grapes have been planted. Also currently being designed and developed are orchards, paddocks, lawn tennis, a gym, a spa and a private villa.

On my last night, I sit in the marble-tiled lounge with my sundowner, watching the sun slip over the Drakenstein mountains. As the peaks melt from gold to pink, nothing moves but two black swans, gliding on the lake. Life, it seems, could hardly be more perfect.

details

When to go
La Residence is open all year.

How to get there
The hotel is in Franschhoek, about one hour by road from Cape Town.

Who to contact
Tel. (+27-15) 793 0150 (central reservations),
e-mail *info@theroyalportfolio.com*
or *reservations@theroyalportfolio.com*,
or go to *www.theroyalportfolio.com*

birkenhead house

Perched on the cliff above Walker Bay is a private hotel

that, like the others in the Royal Portfolio, offers exuberant

décor, elegant comfort and personalised attention.

In the seaside town of Hermanus, there is a sandy cove called Voëlklip Beach. One of the best swimming beaches in the area, it has fond memories for me. It is here that I collected mussels as a child, and surfed my first waves.

Above this beautiful cove is Birkenhead House, which was built by Phil and Liz Biden, who, like me, fell in love with this coast. When the Birkenhead Hotel, the original building on this site, burnt down in 1992, the Bidens bought the land and built their own holiday home. Later, to share its beauty with others, they redeveloped it as a part of their Royal Portfolio – an exclusive set of properties that includes Royal Malewane, near Kruger National Park, La Residence in Franschhoek and the exclusive Birkenhead Villa, next door to the house.

Birkenhead House's grand entrance hall, courtyards and lavish rooms make me feel plushly pampered and privileged, but the staff are so relaxed and friendly that I also feel comfortably at home. Liz Biden is a collector of beautiful artworks and has a wonderful amalgamation of classical, modern and eccentric pieces. I would never have thought of buying a two-metre high cabinet covered in hundreds of seashells, a red and white poodle vase, or a plastic statue of Marilyn Monroe, but in this extraordinary house they look entirely fitting.

The artworks can also be seen in the 11 gracious rooms, which all have twinkling chandeliers, heated marble floors and giant four-poster beds draped with the finest linen. Not least, all have wonderful views across the cyan waters of Walker Bay to mist-shrouded mountains and the horizon.

In keeping with other Royal Portfolio properties, the five-star restaurant is only open to guests. Lunches are served in the courtyard beside the dual-level swimming pool, and dinners are presented on fine china and crystal in the glass-fronted dining room with a view of the sea. The menu changes daily and, in addition to champagne,

Hermanus offers one of the best land-based whale watching sites in the world

oysters and other delectable seaside treats, the most delicious home-made bread and pastries are on offer. The chef, who greets and attends to guests personally, tells me that his cuisine is 'modern African with a mixture of French, Italian and Asian influences'. It certainly is wonderful.

Early one morning, I take a walk along the cliff path, which runs below Birkenhead House, and look up at two iron cannons rusting on the rocks. They are the remains of the Royal Navy vessel *Birkenhead* that was wrecked off this point in 1852, causing the deaths of more than 450 people.

I cross sandy inlets where cormorants perch on the rocks, and step over cool streams that flow into the sea. Voëlklip is part of the Fernkloof Nature Reserve, which stretches from the coast to the rolling mountains that rise up behind the hotel. The walks are wonderful, and I see signs of Cape clawless otter. Fernkloof is also famous for its spectacular array of fynbos flora.

Hermanus offers one of the best land-based whale watching sites in the world, and every year from July to December hundreds of southern right whales travel from their Antarctic feeding grounds to these warmer waters to mate and calve. That afternoon, from the elegant lounge, I sip tea and nibble on cookies and watch these massive mammals as they surge from the water and slap their massive tails with a thunderous splash on its surface.

PREVIOUS SPREAD Birkenhead House perches above Voëlklip Beach, one of Hermanus's finest.

Fit for royalty, a raised bed with fine linen entices guests to rest.

THIS SPREAD The dual-level swimming pool.

Rest a while on a chaise in the his-and-hers bathroom.

Walker Bay is known for its regular visitors – southern right whales.

Prepare yourself for some excellent and imaginative cuisine.

The resort's pool lies at the edge of the ocean, offering guests views across the ever-changing water to the distant horizon.

details

When to go
Birkenhead House is open all year.

How to get there
Hermanus is a 90-minute drive along the N2 from Cape Town.

Who to contact
Tel. (+27-15) 793 0150 (central reservations), e-mail *info@theroyalportfolio.com* or *reservations@theroyalportfolio.com*, or go to *www.theroyalportfolio.com*

grootbos
private nature reserve

This flora-filled reserve on the steep slopes above beautiful

Walker Bay combines great facilities for visitors and a fervent

commitment to the local community.

In 1991, when the Lutzeyer family purchased some 1 750 hectares of overfarmed land along the southern Cape coast, alien infestation was so bad that botanists thought the indigenous fynbos would never recover. Today, world-renowned conservationist Professor David Bellamy regards Grootbos Private Nature Reserve as the best example of biodiversity conservation that he has ever seen. The reserve has also won national and international acclaim for its conservation and social work.

Grootbos is, indeed, a wonderful place. Here, two spectacular five-star lodges, Forest Lodge and Garden Lodge, have been constructed with care in one of the largest milkwood forests in the Western Cape. They offer wide views over Walker Bay, with its annual sightings of southern right whales. Garden Lodge, which caters for families, is built of sandstone and thatch, and lies in a lush and established indigenous garden. The more modern Forest Lodge, built in 2004, has spacious suites that are accessed by cobbled paths that wind through the forest.

The Lutzeyer family are passionate conservationists and established the Grootbos Foundation in 2004. 'Our mission,' said Michael Lutzeyer, 'was to build an enterprise based on the livelihoods of people living in the area.' The lodge now has more than 100 employees and has helped to establish the Green Futures Horticulture and Life Skills College, which trains people from the area in the fields of fynbos landscaping and horticulture.

One of the graduates is Nzuzo Nkhili, who now works at Grootbos as a guide. He took me on a flower safari and, driving along the steep track up the mountainside, I gazed across the ocean to the misty horizon. Beneath us lay the property. The Cape Floral Kingdom is the smallest and most diverse of the world's six flora biomes, with some 10 000 plant species, many of which occur nowhere else. Grootbos itself has 740 species, including 102 that are Vulnerable or Endangered and five that are new to science. Of these, three were discovered by Heiner Lutzeyer, a

Spring is the best time for flowers, although there is always something in bloom, and there are plenty of birds

passionate amateur botanist. These species were discovered in the wake of a fire that spread through the reserve in 2006. 'This is a fire-driven system,' explained Nzuzo. 'Fynbos depends on regular fires to germinate its seeds.'

Spring is the best time for flowers, although there is always something in bloom, and there are plenty of birds, including startlingly beautiful sunbirds. Grootbos has a stable with 22 sure-footed horses which can be used to explore the reserve, if you're not in the mood for walking.

I joined a beach safari to De Kelders (the caves). The rugged limestone cliffs along this stretch of coastline include hall-sized caverns, where there is evidence of San hunter-gatherers who, for centuries, spent the dry summer months here, living on a diet of seafood. There are plenty of signs of other life too, including cormorants, seals and great white sharks, which may be seen by the brave from cages off nearby Dyer Island.

I visit Grootbos often, and each occasion reveals a new and delightful development. This time, it was the launch of Spaces for Sport, with five soccer fields, a clubhouse and the first FIFA-standard artificial soccer pitch in South Africa. These were prompted by Michael Lutzeyer, who, in a 2004 visit to the nearby fishing village of Gansbaai, noticed that 17 soccer clubs all used one dusty pitch. He obtained funding and donations of land, and the soccer players now have decent facilities. 'It all goes to show just how much positive influence tourism can have on local communities and their quality of life,' said Michael.

PREVIOUS SPREAD There's a rich patchwork of flora at Grootbos.

Modern Forest Lodge has a soaring roof and never-ending views.

THIS SPREAD Investigating the fynbos for flowers.

Newly refurbished Forest Lodge offers tranquil respite from everyday life.

There's a cooling pool in which to wallow after a day in the sun.

There's always lots to investigate at Walker Bay, from breathtaking views to a multi-specied marine life.

There's nothing better than waking in a comfortable bed to a view across an ever-changing ocean.

details

When to go
Fynbos, attractive all year, is most vibrant in spring. The best time to see the whales and sharks is between April and October.

How to get there
Grootbos is a 90-minute drive from Cape Town. Take the N2, then the turn-off to Hermanus and follow the signposts to Stanford.

Who to contact
Tel. (+27-28) 384 8000,
e-mail info@grootbos.co.za
or go to www.grootbos.com

arniston
spa hotel

Tucked snugly above a beautiful curved bay, this slow-paced and serene getaway for romantics and lovers of nature lies a short hop from Africa's southernmost tip.

The hotel is set in one of
the Cape's most beautiful
locations, a small fishing
village named after an East
Indiaman ship that
sank here in 1815

PREVIOUS SPREAD Poised between sea and sky, Arniston glows
and twinkles in the early evening light.

THIS SPREAD Fishermen have launched their boats into this bay
for over two centuries.

Unwinding at the Ginkgo Health and Wellness Spa.

The central courtyard is a suntrap, enticing guests to lie poolside.

Arniston is undeniably beautiful, with its long white-sand
beaches and endless ocean in every shade of blue.

The hotel has 60 elegantly decorated en-suite rooms.

It's a relaxed two-hours' drive from Cape Town to Arniston and, beneath the baking sun, I head over Sir Lowry's Pass and into the rolling landscape of the Overberg. I check into the Arniston Spa Hotel, then head off to Roman Beach and its inviting turquoise water. Puffy white clouds scud across the deep-blue sky and I wade into the warm Indian Ocean.

After bodysurfing the breakers, I stroll down to the harbour, where the fishing boats are returning from their day at sea. 'In the past, we used to catch plenty of fish,' says Harry Mitchell, unfastening his yellow oilskin. 'But these days the fishing is not so good and we are lucky to get 10 or 20 kilograms,' he says wistfully.

The Arniston Spa Hotel is set in one of the Cape's most beautiful locations, a small fishing village named after an East Indiaman ship that sank here in 1815, with a loss of 372 lives. The hotel has 60 elegantly decorated en-suite rooms. The deluxe ocean-facing units have private balconies, while the patio-facing rooms open on to the swimming pool area.

The bar area has big-screen televisions and two aquariums filled with local sea fish. There are conference facilities for up to 100 delegates and the hotel is also a popular wedding venue. At the Ginkgo Health and Wellness Spa, the menu lists numerous body treatments and massages, including a *rasul* (an Arabic cleansing ritual), a hydrotherapy bath, two saunas and a soothing tranquillity lounge.

Meals here naturally focus on seafood. The fresh fish is bought straight from the boats, and shellfish, oysters and lobsters are always available. The menu also has Cape Malay dishes and traditional South African cuisine, complemented by an award-winning list of local wines. The cosy wine cellar can host up to 34 people for a dining experience with a difference.

There are lots of activities to work off your meals, including fishing, mountain-biking, snorkelling, hiking, bird- and whale-watching, squash, tennis and horseriding. Arniston's beautiful beaches are ideal for swimming and there's a stretch of coastal sand dunes to explore, as well as the cave called Waenhuiskrans, which is only accessible at low tide. In winter, southern right whales are often sighted in the bay.

This slow-paced town is famous for the friendly fishing village of Kassiesbaai, with its distinctive white-washed, thatched cottages. The cluster of 200-year-old houses has been declared a national monument. Here, guests can enjoy a traditional candlelit evening meal in one of the fishermen's houses.

The surrounding area is also worth investigating. Nearby Bredasdorp has interesting arts-and-crafts shops, a golf course and a shipwreck museum; De Hoop and De Mond nature reserves have unspoilt coastal trails; and Cape Agulhas, the southernmost tip of Africa, is a big attraction.

After a memorable dinner of calamari steak, followed by grilled yellowtail served with a lemon-butter sauce, vegetables and creamy mashed potatoes, I sleep deeply. Waking to a golden sunrise, I set off to visit the coastal cave of Waenhuiskrans. I clamber carefully along the slippery shoreline and locate the small entrance in the rocks where I squeeze through into the cavernous lime-green interior. It's almost low tide and I indulge in some macro photography, capturing images of the periwinkles, starfish and sea anemones in the exposed rock pools. Just offshore, a whale and its baby swim slowly past.

details

When to go
Arniston is a year-round destination. The best time for whale-watching is between July and October.

How to get there
Arniston is just over two hours by road from Cape Town. Take the N2 highway over Sir Lowry's Pass and turn off onto the R316 at Caledon. After passing through Bredasdorp, continue for a further 25 kilometres to Arniston.

Who to contact
Tel. (+27-28) 445 9000,
e-mail *info@arnistonhotel.com*
or go to *www.arnistonhotel.com*

phantom forest
eco reserve

Fairytale suites and a variety of dining delights offer stressed

guests a tranquil haven in the forests of Knysna.

Knysna lies at the heart of the Garden Route, and its famous lagoon has been a harbour for countless sailing ships. Today, the town bustles with visitors, traffic and restaurants. But, in the forest high above lagoon's northern shore, there's a harbour of a different sort – one in which busy people can toss aside the cares of the world.

We realise we are in for a unique experience from the moment we drive through the gated entrance, where we are greeted by wrought-iron warthogs perched atop a penny-farthing bicycle. Leaving our car in a guarded parking lot, we are transported into a surreal world of fantasy.

Our room is a quaint wood-and-shingle tree house with a definite Hansel and Gretel air, and the fairytale impression is carried through into the cosy, luxurious interior. The rooms, discreetly spaced along a boardwalk that meanders for more than a kilometre through the forest, are furnished by with genuine style by owner Kit Stewart, and are adorned with colourful knick-knacks and fabrics collected on her travels abroad, particularly to India and Morocco. Bathrooms are glass-walled extravagances facing on to undisturbed forest, and it is not unusual to see Knysna turacos or even blue duiker while bathing each morning. For birders, Phantom Forest offers more than 160 species, including regular sightings of 'mega-tick' narina trogons.

After a delicious meal, I tell Kit that she should rename her lodge Gastronome Forest, so spectacular is the cuisine in this award-winning eco-reserve. 'It is the major attraction here,' she laughs. However, after two days in the lodge, we realise that there is far more on offer than just food. There are lots of other guests, despite it being April and almost the low season here, and they are up to all sorts of activities during the day. There are forest trails to hike, we are told, and canoeing on the river and lagoon. And, being located in the heart of the spectacular Garden Route, Phantom Forest is an ideal base from which to explore this lush region.

For those visitors looking for relaxation rather than rambling, and we were among them, the lodge offers the ideal place to simply unwind. There are numerous nooks and crannies in which to curl up with a good book and the attentive staff will ensure one is never without a cup of herbal tea, a mug of coffee, an iced cocktail or a bottle of wine from the award-winning wine list.

There is also a fully equipped 'body boma' or stress-release centre offering an array of treatments, from reiki massage, reflexology and aromatherapy, mud-baths and body wraps … plus others I'd never heard of, but sounded sumptuous.

However, Phantom Forest is more than a mere sensory experience. It is also an award-winning eco-establishment. While ecotourism has become a much used (and abused) buzz-word in tourism throughout the world, this lodge has embraced its philosophy and principles wholeheartedly. The Phantom Forest Project, started in 1997, is based on the concept of conservation funded by limited, sympathetic development. The lodge is set in a 147-hectare private nature reserve comprising three unique biospheres – afromontane forest, Cape coastal fynbos and estuarine wetland – and all development has been carried out according to strict guidelines overseen by a professional conservation trust.

Alien vegetation was cleared by hand and the timber was used in the construction of the lodge. All indigenous plants that were lifted to make way for the building phase were dug up and replanted once construction was completed. In addition, all the lodge's waste water is cycled through their own sewage plant then pumped up to reedbeds, where it eventually filters back into the ground as clean re-usable water.

As I sit on a soft couch with view of the forest and a glass of delicious wine in my hand, it is comforting to know that my footprint here will be a small one. Sighing, I settle back on the cushions.

PREVIOUS SPREAD Gentle lighting at the lodge reflects in the pool, casting a tranquil glow on the surrounding forest.

THIS SPREAD The bathroom and its huge windows offer seamless views of the surrounding vegetation and its inhabitants.

Rustic charm combines with modern sophistication and jewel colours to make a truly fairytale retreat.

Phantom Forest's cuisine is legendary.

The perfect setting for an evening chat, with Moroccan treasures, cosy cushions and the gentle lap of the water in the pool.

The bubble barrel and a glass of chilled champagne is the ideal way to relax after a day spent exploring the forest.

PHANTOM FOREST

The rooms, discreetly spaced along a boardwalk that meanders for more than a kilometre through the forest, are furnished with style

details

When to go
Phantom Forest is open all year.

How to get there
The lodge is seven kilometres beyond Knysna on the road to Cape Town. Daily scheduled flights link all the major centres in South Africa with nearby George, where a car may be hired for the scenic drive to Knysna via Wilderness and part of the Garden Route.

Who to contact
Tel. (+27-44) 386 0046,
e-mail *phantomforest@mweb.co.za*
or go to *www.phantomforest.com*

western cape

African penguins at Boulders Beach.

HERMAN VAN DEN BERG

SPEND A FEW DAYS exploring the vibrant and scenically splendid city of Cape Town, with its busy waterfront area, iconic Table Mountain and white beaches. A short distance out of town lie the winelands, where you can sample world-famous Cape vintages in stunning settings beneath craggy mountains. Following the coastline, stop for a night in the Hermanus and Gansbaai area, then continue to the Garden Route. Whales, flowers and forests will be your companions on this journey, as you pass beautiful seaside towns such as Knysna and Plettenberg Bay. Alternatively, follow the N7 from Cape Town, and head along the West Coast, where quaint fishing villages and wild spring flowers will delight you.

For itinerary suggestions, contact:
AFRICA GEOGRAPHIC TRAVEL
Tel. (+27-21) 762 2180
E-mail *travel@africageographic.com*
Website *www.africageographictravel.com*

Cape Town

Table Mountain This iconic symbol of Cape Town offers great hiking and climbing routes, and there is a cable-car ride for the less energetic. Both of these will offer fantastic views of the city and beyond.

Waterfront The V&A Waterfront offers a variety of activities, from shopping in its bustling mall to lunching on the deck while watching the boats and seals, or visiting the Two Oceans Aquarium.

Robben Island The island is famous for the maximum-security prison that was used during the years of apartheid and, of course, for Nelson Mandela – one of its best-known inmates. Today it is a World Heritage Site and visitors can take a guided historical tour of the island and museum. (The ferry leaves from the V&A Waterfront.)

Kirstenbosch Botanical Gardens This 528-hectare floral sanctuary lies beneath the eastern slopes of Table Mountain. The abundance of birdlife, plants and grassed areas provide an idyllic setting for a stroll or a picnic. In summer, concerts are held on the lawns. Two restaurants provide refreshments.

Chapman's Peak Drive This scenic marine drive was hewn into the side of the mountain almost 100 years ago, and winds between Hout Bay and Noordhoek. There are plenty of viewpoints for photos or a picnic, with spectacular scenery.

Penguins at Boulders Beach Just south of Simon's Town is Boulders Beach, where a colony of African penguins has made its home between the rocks and indigenous bushes. The area is protected, allowing visitors to view the birds in their natural habitat.

Cape Point Cape Point, or the Cape of Good Hope, situated at the southern tip of Africa, is a place notorious for its treacherous seas, which have engulfed many ships rounding its peninsula. This area forms part of the Table Mountain National Park and is home to a wealth of flora and abundant wildlife, including ostriches. There are numerous walking trails, beaches and picnic spots in the reserve.

Kirstenbosch National Botanical Gardens.

DAVID ROGERS (2)

The Winelands

Cape Town and the Western Cape are world-renowned for their scenic vineyards and award-winning wines. Famous wine routes include Constantia, Durbanville, Helderberg, Overberg, Franschhoek, Paarl, Stellenbosch, Tulbagh and Robertson. Many of the estates have shops, restaurants and picnic facilities.

Whale-watching

Many seaside villages offer amazing land-based whale-watching experiences. The best time to visit is between October and January, when southern right and other whales visit this coast. In Hermanus, the whale crier, the first in the world, patrols the streets during the whale season, informing visitors about the best places to view these giant mammals.

West Coast

The West Coast is renowned for its spectacular displays of wildflowers that emerge in spring to carpet the landscape with blooms in shades of orange, yellow, purple, cream and pink. There are more than 8 600 species of flowers in the area, of which 68 per cent occur nowhere else on earth. The West Coast National Park offers two scenic backdrops to the floral displays in the fascinating rock formations of the Postberg peninsula, and the turquoise waters of the 15-kilometre-long Langebaan Lagoon.

Swartberg mountains, Route 62.

In Darling, popular local entertainer Pieter-Dirk Uys has created a theatre in the old railway station building, where performances are regularly held.

Garden Route

The Garden Route is a coastal corridor on South Africa's southern coast, where ancient forests, rivers, wetlands, dunes, beaches, lakes, mountains and indigenous fynbos merge to form a landscape of magical beauty. Numerous hiking trails are found here, including the well-known Otter Trail, which winds more than 40 kilometres through shady forests and dramatic coastal scenery. En route is Knysna, a pretty holiday resort with two jutting cliffs, The Heads, protecting its lagoon.

Route 62

Route 62 links Cape Town with Port Elizabeth, meandering through Oudtshoorn, the ostrich capital of the Little Karoo, farmlands, historic mission towns, fruit orchards and vineyards. It is also a preferred destination for self-drive holidays in South Africa, with lots to see and do on the journey.

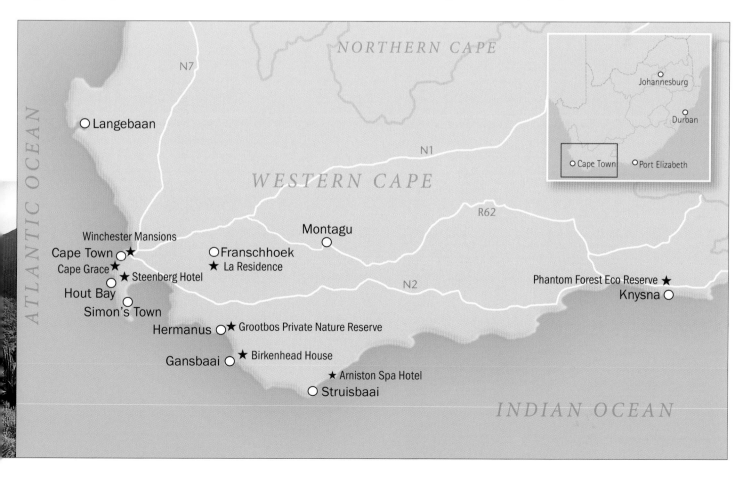

JEREMY JOWELL (3)

DARYL BALFOUR

where forest & ocean meet

eastern cape

Tsitsikamma National Park.
DAVID ROGERS

Once the setting of fierce frontier battles between the indigenous Xhosa people and European settlers, the Eastern Cape is now home to a burgeoning number of wildlife sanctuaries. And, with its lush and diverse scenery, visitors to this region can see herds of elephants, elusive rhinos and a host of antelope species in the morning, and stroll along pristine sandy beaches in the afternoon.

riverbend
lodge

From your suite, you can watch as a herd of elephants

strolls silently in single file to the lodge's waterhole.

[The elephants] amble over and feed around us, stuffing leaves and grass into their mouths. Some strip off chunks of cactus

PREVIOUS SPREAD Facing outwards, overlooking the reserve, each suite is completely private.

Rhinos silhouetted against a darkening sky.

THIS SPREAD The rooms are elegant, yet comfortable.

The elephants at RiverBend are good-natured.

Sundowners in a superb setting.

Deep couches in the main sitting room encourage visitors to relax with a book from the lodge's large library.

Young children are welcome at RiverBend.

It's my first morning at RiverBend Lodge and I wake long before dawn. The sky is still dark and the birds have just begun to twitter. Joining the ranger on the Land Rover, we drive along a dust road and watch a jackal slink away into the bushes.

The horizon brightens and we see, in the distance, a 50-strong herd of elephants approaching. They amble over and graze around us, stuffing leaves and grass into their mouths. Some strip off chunks of cactus. Occasionally the beasts rumble and trumpet, communicating with each other. 'Our elephants have a reputation for being extremely good-natured and are completely relaxed in our presence,' whispers ranger Justin Davies, as a large male stands unperturbed just a metre from our vehicle.

Flanked by the Zuurberg Mountains, RiverBend Lodge is situated in the malaria-free 14 000-hectare Nyathi private concession area of the Addo Elephant National Park. The focus here is on personal attention and tailor-made safaris. As manager Marius Malherbe said when I arrived, 'We take a maximum of six people per vehicle. The game drive starts when they're ready, and the ranger will stop whenever they want to observe the animals more closely.'

Other activities at the lodge include guided walks, birdwatching, stargazing (the night skies are spectacular) and photographic safaris. Guests can also learn about the medicinal value of plants or take a self-guided historical tour to the nearby battlefields. RiverBend's Vitality Studio offers a range of treatments, including facials, reflexology, manicures and massage.

Accommodation is in eight tastefully designed suites, each equipped with satellite television and a spacious en-suite bathroom, or the private Long Hope Villa – the perfect destination for a family safari. Children of all ages are welcome. Family suites have interleading rooms and there is a playroom filled with toys, books, games and DVDs. Child-minders are in attendance should you want to relax without the children or enjoy a intimate dinner.

Food plays a pivotal role here, and the cuisine is a blend of traditional dishes and pan-African cuisine, accompanied by South Africa's finest wines. Sitting down to lunch, I peruse the menu that consists of 15 tempting choices. I settle for Chinese vegetable spring rolls with a sweet chilli sauce.

Later, after an hour at the pool, I set out on a late afternoon game drive. In addition to large numbers of elephants, there are more than 300 species of birds, black rhino, zebra, warthog, eland, kudu, red hartebeest, and the occasional leopard in the concession. I'm told that the lodge is proudly associated with the Landmark Foundation, which spearheads leopard-conservation initiatives in the Eastern Cape. We stop for sundowners overlooking a green valley with the majestic Zuurberg Mountains in the distance.

The weekend flies past and on the last afternoon we take a game drive in Intsomi Private Game Reserve, to which RiverBend guests have exclusive access. A family of giraffes stands like statues, watching us warily. We're also lucky to spot two white rhinos that run away up a hillside. They stop on top, showing me their profile. Quickly, before they move off, I photograph the the huge beasts silhouetted against the sky.

details

When to go
RiverBend is a year-round destination. May and September are especially good months as the weather is mild and the vegetation is lush. Temperatures can become very high in October and February.

How to get there
RiverBend Lodge is a one-hour drive from Port Elizabeth. Take the N2 towards Grahamstown and the R335 off-ramp marked Motherwell. Continue along this road until you reach the village of Addo. Proceed for a further 11.5 kilometres, then turn left onto a dirt road to Zuurberg. RiverBend's gates lie four kilometres further on.

Who to contact
Tel. (+27-42) 233 8000,
e-mail *reservations@riverbendlodge.co.za*
or go to *www.riverbendlodge.co.za*

camp figtree

The mountain views from this lovely lodge are so grand

that they impress even visitors from Switzerland.

From the veranda of the main lodge building, you can see to the distant horizon in every direction

PREVIOUS SPREAD This is elephant country.
Weather permitting, dinner is served around a roaring fire in the boma.

THIS SPREAD Evening game drives include a stop for sundowners.

It's easy to lose yourself in the view from the lodge's veranda.

Crisp linens, locally wrought furniture and outsized beds guarantee a restful stay.

From the hilltop pool, the Zuurberg mountains roll and tumble into the distance.

From the aptly named 'chill deck', the vegetation literally falls away beneath you.

Paging through the camp guest book, I am intrigued by the number of visitors from Switzerland – and their awed comments about the mountain views from their rooms. Looking out of the window, I realise that Swiss views, no matter how spectacular, could never compare with that before me – the Zuurberg mountains rolling into the distance, the massive wild fig trees shading the old Cape colonial-style lodge buildings, and the lush green thicket vegetation that carpets the hills. Come winter, there could even be snow on the distant peaks …

The drive to Camp Figtree from nearby Addo Elephant National Park winds up a mountain track to the uppermost heights of one of these verdant mountains, and the views from virtually every nook or cranny of the lodge are panoramic. From the veranda of the main lodge building, you can see to the distant horizon in every direction. From the aptly named 'chill deck', the vegetation literally falls away beneath you. There are even spectacular vistas to be had from your bed, or your bathtub.

The lodge is designed in Cape colonial style, with roots that are entwined with the heritage of its owners, Clyde and Marijke Niven. Clyde is the great-grandson of Sir Percy Fitzpatrick, acclaimed author of *Jock of the Bushveld*, and memorabilia dating back to his ancestor's pioneering days is scattered throughout the buildings. Framed enlargements of old black-and-white photographs hang on the corrugated-iron and wood-panelled walls, and leather-bound, limited-edition reprints of his famous book are available for reading in all the rooms. Sir Percy's daughter, Cecily Niven – Clyde's grand-mother – farmed in the district until her death at the age of 90.

There are two accommodation options for guests at Camp Figtree. In the main camp, the charming corrugated-iron cottages have spacious en-suite bathrooms and mosquito-netted four-poster beds. A separate, tented camp offers traditional Hemingway style, albeit with a lot more finesse and comfort than Ernest would have experienced. All the rooms are designed to ensure complete privacy from their neighbours, and there are beautiful views from every one. I eye the stack of books and the comfortable chairs, and it crosses my mind that Camp Figtree would be the perfect place for a convalescence, with its fresh mountain air, soothing views and excellent but unobtrusive service.

Later, in the dining room, I am extremely impressed by both the quality and quantity of the fine cuisine on offer. We tuck in, and notice that the chef emerges personally from the kitchen to inves-tigate when plates are returned not completely empty! There's also an outdoor boma where, weather permitting, tables bedecked with fine linen and sparkling china are set out around the fire.

Camp Figtree is ideally situated to use as a base to explore the area. The Addo park is a short drive away and open game-viewing vehicles are available from the lodge for a guided tour of the reserve. Horseback safaris in the park are also an option, while, for the more adventurous, an elephant-back safari can fill a morning or afternoon. From the lodge, you can explore the surroundings on mountain bikes or on foot – but beware, all paths lead downhill from the camp, with a corresponding uphill return! But, judging by the comments in the guest book, the vast majority of visitors seemed to enjoy Camp Figtree the way we did – for its relaxed atmosphere, stunning views, good food and wonderful, tranquil ambience.

details

When to go
Camp Figtree is open all year. Conditions can be cold during June and July, but blazing fires in the lodge are sure to take the edge off the weather. Nearby Addo Elephant National Park, renowned for its elephant population, is also open all year.

How to get there
Daily scheduled domestic flights connect all major South African cities to Port Elizabeth, from where it is an easy drive of about an hour to Camp Figtree.

Who to contact
Tel. (+27-82) 659 0847,
e-mail *reservations@campfigtree.com*
or go to *www.campfigtree.com*

intsomi
forest lodge

Here, in the Woody Cape wilderness – a sanctuary of

whispering forests, a host of wildlife and coastal dunes that were

once home to ancient Khoisan settlements – is a serene lodge.

A golden glow colours the fields and a kite hovers in the air above us. Bird Island's lighthouse blinks in the distance

A cool breeze whistles through the trees as I drive along the twisting road to Intsomi Forest Lodge. As I arrive, I step out of my car and breathe deeply, inhaling the fresh fragrance of the forest.

Intsomi's eco-guide Kate Muller is there to greet me. 'There's so much variety here,' she tells me. 'Pristine indigenous forest meets the vast Alexandria coastal dunefield, the largest shifting dunefield in the southern hemisphere. And, driving down the green Langevlakte valley, you can watch antelope graze. Three worlds collide with amazing beauty and a stunning variety of life.'

Intsomi Forest lodge is situated in the Woody Cape Wilderness Area, part of the coastal section of the Addo Elephant National Park. In this unique setting, you can find rare tree-living dassies, blue duikers and endangered oribis. The beautiful birdlife includes Knysna turacos, narina trogons, African crowned eagles, chorister robin-chats and 'bush musicians' (dark-backed weavers).

The lodge is as magical as the forest that surrounds it. The architecture blends with the natural surroundings with high floating ceilings, rustic earth colours and open plan spaces. The eight suites are built predominantly of wood and glass. These stylish units have glass walls on three sides that slide open to allow you to enjoy the sights and sounds of the forest from the comfort of your bed. Wooden walkways wind through the foliage, linking the suites to the main lodge, which contains a dining area, lounge, boardroom, swimming pool, sundeck and colourful curio shop. Sundowners are usually enjoyed on the deck, which overlooks a waterhole often visited by animals intent on getting their own evening drink. Dinners are a sumptuous affair and are served either in the main dining area or on the deck, accompanied by fine South African wines. And then there are always massage and beauty treatments to be enjoyed within the sanctuary of the forest.

The area around the lodge is a haven for hikers, with both easy and challenging walks through the forest and along the Alexandria coastal dunefields. These dunes stretch for 50 kilometres from the Sundays River to Woody Cape, and shelter many Khoisan shell middens, which are a must-see.

I enjoy an afternoon siesta and awake feeling refreshed. All is quiet as I step onto my veranda, except for the chirping of birds. Later, I join Kate on a sunset drive along Lookout Drive. 'Let me show you this flower,' she says, stopping the vehicle. 'It's a forest gardenia and has a wonderful smell. I've been waiting five months for it to bloom. Mmmm,' she says, inhaling deeply.

We drive through the vast green Langevlakte valley, stopping to watch a herd of hartebeest grazing beside zebras and a lone gemsbok. Five buffaloes approach and eyeball us from just a few metres away. At the top of a hill, we gaze down to the dunefield as the sun breaks through, creating pastel-coloured patterns in the sky. A golden glow colours the fields and a kite hovers in the air above us. Bird Island's lighthouse blinks in the distance. It's chilly by the time we get back to the lodge, so a mug of hot chocolate spiked with Amarula liqueur is a welcome surprise.

The next morning I wake early and set off with Kate for a dawn outing to the dunes. We drive past the coastal vegetation to the middens – vast piles of seashells left by the nomadic Khoisan people who made their living from the sea many centuries ago. We take off our boots and walk along the deserted beach.

'This coast gets many whales in season,' says Kate, 'and sometimes I have stood in the surf and watched a school of 200 dolphins glide past in the breakers. This landscape is where the Khoisan lived and worked and ate. Can you imagine living permanently in this paradise?'

White waves wash in from the Indian Ocean and, stripping off my clothes, I dive into the warm frothy surf for a sunrise swim.

PREVIOUS SPREAD Lost in admiration for the beautiful Alexandria coastal dunefield, the largest in the southern hemisphere.

THIS SPREAD The suites are cosily furnished with wood and textured fabrics in rich colours.

A huge waterboom stands sentinel in the forest.

The lounge at Intsomi.

Long ago, Khoisan people lived among these dunes, and seashell middens attest to their lifestyle.

Wooden walkways link the suites to the main lodge and its pool deck.

details

When to go
Intsomi Forest Lodge is a year-round destination. The period between September and November is the best time for whale-watching in Algoa Bay and the weather is warm and mild during these months.

How to get there
From Port Elizabeth, take the N2 towards Grahamstown, then take the R72 turnoff to Port Alfred. Immediately prior to entering Alexandria, turn right at the 'Kaba/Grootvlei' sign, drive through a security boom and follow the signs for 'Intsomi Forest Lodge/Woody Cape Wilderness Section'. Pass the entrance to the nature reserve and turn right at the 'Intsomi Forest Lodge' sign.

Who to contact
Tel. (+27-46) 653 8903/4/5, e-mail *info@intsomi.com* or go to *www.intsomi.co.za*

oceana beach
& wildlife reserve

There are few luxury reserves that offer the

opportunity to view whales as well as nyala, buffalo

and rhino. Oceana is a five-star lodge in every sense.

I wake early on my first morning at the Oceana Beach and Wildlife Reserve and lie in bed watching streaks of cloud turn pink over the Indian Ocean. Still half asleep, I gather up my gear and head to the beach. There's not a soul in sight as I stroll along the shore, collecting stones and shells. A weak sun appears through the sea mist and I spot a dolphin surfing in the breakers.

The sand dunes here are spectacular and, armed with my camera, I meander through them, admiring the colourful contrasts and rippled patterns in the dawn light. On the crest of a dune, I click away at the dainty tracks left by an oystercatcher. This place is a photographer's dream.

Surrounded by 1 000 hectares of lush vegetation and rolling grasslands, Oceana Beach and Wildlife Reserve is situated near Port Alfred in the Eastern Cape. This ultra-luxurious lodge has a panoramic view over a pristine white beach to the Indian Ocean, prompting some guests to describe the region as 'the most beautiful place on earth'.

There are seven stylish suites with wrap-around balconies, flat-screen televisions, and 'his and hers' bathrooms with underfloor heating, a spa bath and a double shower. A separate Ocean House comprises three en-suite bedrooms, a kitchen and a cosy lounge with a fireplace. This cottage is the ideal retreat for small groups or families.

The lodge has a games room with a pool table, computer facilities, a shuffle board and board games. There is also a library, an elegant dining room, a swimming pool and a sundeck. A waterhole below the veranda is well supported by wildlife. The Oceana Wellness Centre, with a gym, steam room and spa, offers a wide range of beauty and massage treatments.

Since its opening in 2007, Oceana has become extremely popular with both local and international visitors. 'Some guests prefer the bush, while others like the beach, so it's great to be able to offer a combination of both,' says manager Karen Eggers. 'We are a unique lodge because there's nowhere else in South Africa where you can watch wildlife and then take a walk along a beautiful beach.'

Activities are varied and Oceana offers the best of both bush attractions and ocean adventures. Take your pick from game drives, hiking, nature walks, mountain-biking, fishing, stargazing, romantic beach picnics and whale-watching in season, when humpbacks and southern rights are regularly sighted. For golf fanatics, there is a championship course not far away, and a putting green on the lodge's helipad.

After a back and neck massage at the spa, I relax at the pool, then head out on an afternoon game drive. We see bontebok, sable and waterbuck, the distinctive white circles on their rears clearly visible. We also spot wildebeest, buffalo, black impala, giraffes and a herd of zebras. High on a hill, we find two white rhinos grazing on green grass. As if on cue, the sun breaks through, bathing the bulky animals in a soft orange light. 'The female is pregnant so we will be getting a new addition quite soon,' says our guide.

In a clearing, we stop for sundowners and sip our gin and tonics, looking out to the glistening blue waters of a crescent-shaped bay. The golden ball of the sun sinks behind distant mountains – it's a spectacular sight.

The executive chef at Oceana has 28 years of experience and the cuisine, a fusion of South African and European traditions, is decidedly five-star. At dinner, I feast on grilled sole served with a prawn mousse and steamed vegetables. Dessert arrives and my mouth waters as I taste the decadent Lindt chocolate tart.

Replete, I amble back to my suite and open the sliding doors to the veranda. After a spot of stargazing, sleep comes easily, accompanied by the gentle murmur of the ocean.

PREVIOUS SPREAD Pretty chandeliers illuminate the spacious, comfortable suites.

Zebras keep an eye on the visitors.

THIS SPREAD A relaxing massage in a bush-and-beach setting.

Oceana's guests have called this region 'the most beautiful place on earth'.

An inky sky highlights the lodge's cosiness.

A giraffe, silhouetted against the clouds.

All meals at Oceana are prepared by an accomplished chef.

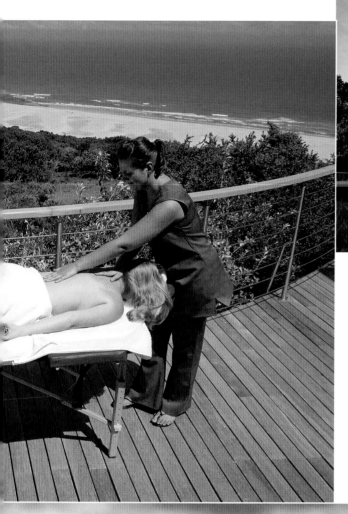

On the crest of a dune, I click away at the dainty tracks left by an oystercatcher. This place is a photographer's dream

details

When to go
Temperatures are relatively mild all year and there is no bad time to visit this stretch of the Eastern Cape. The best months for whale sightings are between September and November.

How to get there
Oceana is situated on the R72, eight kilometres north-east of Port Alfred, which is halfway between Port Elizabeth and East London.

Who to contact
Tel. (+27-83) 616 0605,
e-mail *reservations@oceanareserve.com*
or go to *www.oceanareserve.com*

samara
private game reserve

Home to creatures once hunted to extinction in the area, this reserve and its gracious owners offer a wildlife experience second to none.

Seven sets of amber eyes watch closely as we inch towards the family of cheetahs, careful not to make any sudden move that might spook the cats and send them scattering into the dense Karoo scrub. Sibella, the matriarch of the clan and reputed to be the first cheetah returned to the Great Karoo in 125 years, appears far more nonchalant about our presence than her one-year-old offspring, which bare their fangs and edge nearer to mum as we get closer.

Once we still our approach and started clicking away with cameras, the cheetahs settle, return to their grooming, and start purring contentedly. I have photographed countless cheetahs over the years, but never before have I done so on foot, or at such close range.

Close encounters with cheetahs are just one of the treats that await visitors to the 28 000-hectare Samara Private Game Reserve, one of the largest private reserves in South Africa. Spread beneath the Sneeuberg mountains, less than an hour's drive from the quaint Karoo town of Graaff-Reinet, the reserve is the dream-child of UK businessman Mark Tompkins and his South African wife, Sarah. Perhaps most significantly, it is home to the first cheetahs re-introduced to the Great Karoo since the species was hunted to extinction in the area more than 125 years ago. Sibella has produced three litters since being brought here from the De Wildt Cheetah and Wildlife Trust near Pretoria. Today the cheetah population numbers 14.

Although the cheetahs are the stars of Samara, they are not its only attractions. Since 1997, the Tompkins' main objective has been to realise the potential of this land both as an area of outstanding natural diversity – its 28 000 hectares encompass four of South Africa's seven major vegetation biomes – and as a home to re-introduced species that once roamed freely here. Today, it is a haven for the rare Cape mountain zebra, and South Africa's national bird, the blue crane. Additionally, Burchell's zebras, white rhinos, giraffes, buffaloes, greater kudu, oryx, red hartebeest, black

Close encounters with cheetahs are just one of the treats that await visitors

wildebeest, eland, reedbuck, springbok, common duiker and steenbok were all seen during our brief stay.

Samara has two accommodation options. Karoo Lodge is a gracious colonial homestead with deeply shaded verandas. A second homestead, The Manor at Samara, will soon be in operation. Dating back to the 19th century, the painstakingly refurbished Karoo Lodge farmhouse is tastefully decorated in a warm, luxurious style. It has three en-suite bedrooms, with another three free-standing suites beneath shady acacias in the grounds. We felt completely at home. Discreet but attentive service took care of our every need, be it a cup of Earl Grey tea or a late-morning sandwich after returning from an extended game drive.

Mealtimes were a gastronomic treat, with a fusion of traditional South African, classic French and a modern Karoo influence, with aromatic Karoo lamb a speciality, of course.

Although their main focus is the South African safari experience, the Tompkins recognise their social responsibilities. To this end, at least 90 per cent of their staff are from the local community, while children from disadvantaged backgrounds attend regular environmental-education programmes, such as the planting of spekboom trees.

Early one morning, we drive onto the high plateau. Here we enjoy coffee, home-made rusks and freshly baked scones and watch the golden rays of the rising sun creep across the Plains of Camdeboo. From the rocky crevices, baboons bark their greetings and kestrels and jackal buzzards soar on the thermals.

PREVIOUS SPREAD Samara Private Game Reserve lies beneath the ancient Sneeuberg mountains. The sanctuary is home to the first cheetahs in the Great Karoo for more than a century.

THIS SPREAD Breakfast overlooking the never-ending plains.

Fine cuisine is served with a smile.

The high-ceilinged rooms at Karoo Lodge are furnished with quiet elegance and attention to detail.

As the sun sets, lanterns are lit to illuminate the lodge.

A few members of Samara's resident cheetah population.

details

When to go
Samara is open all year. Temperatures in winter (from May to July) can be low, with snow often falling on the surrounding peaks.

How to get there
Samara is about three hours by road from Port Elizabeth or an hour from the picturesque town of Graaff-Reinet. Charter flights can be arranged to the reserve's own airstrip.

Who to contact
Tel. (+27-49) 891 0558,
e-mail *reservations@samara.co.za*
or go to *www.samara.co.za*

mount camdeboo
private game reserve

Feel the breeze, admire the wide-open scenery and gaze in awe at the wealth of wildlife at this beautiful Karoo reserve, the realisation of a visionary's dream.

MOUNT CAMDEBOO

PREVIOUS SPREAD Rare Cape mountain zebras graze beneath the rolling Sneeuberg mountains.

THIS SPREAD Stone walls and reed ceilings combine quirkily with rich furnishings and swathed beds.

Three old homesteads (this is Hillside Manor) have been lovingly restored.

Mount Camdeboo's cuisine is Karoo-style, with a modern twist.

Tea is served beside the pool.

Cosy lanterns used in the evening create a romantic atmosphere.

Logie Buchanan was a man with a dream. In 1996, the Cape Town businessman, farmer and philanthropist purchased a struggling farm named Mount Pleasant in the Great Karoo, then went on to accumulate another five neighbouring properties of sprawling valleys and mountain plateaus in the Sneeuberg mountains near historic Graaff Reinet. His dream? To restore the dying land to health for his family. However, before his plans could be realised, Logie passed away. Now, his son Iain is making sure that his dad did not dream in vain.

'My dad brought me here shortly after my 14th birthday. I thought we were going on another camping trip in the mountains. Then, after climbing onto a ridge, he spread his arms and told me that we owned the land before us!

'This was to be a family getaway place, a corner of Africa that my dad wanted to restore,' Iain told us as we perched on a rocky promontory overlooking what he now calls the Mount Camdeboo Private Game Reserve.

Since taking over the land, Iain has painstakingly restored three colonial homesteads – Camdeboo, Courtyard and Hillside manors. Furnished in plush but homely farmhouse style, they offer visitors slick, discreet service and exemplary cuisine in traditional Karoo style with a modern twist.

Outside, Iain has removed fences and re-introduced animals that historically roamed the area. Today, the reserve teems with greater kudu, as well as Cape mountain zebras, disease-free Cape buffaloes, giraffes, herds of eland, black wildebeest, springbok, blesbok, red hartebeest, common duiker and Burchell's zebras. There are also cheetahs, black-backed jackals and white rhinos. Nocturnal animals include aardvarks and aardwolves, as well as springhares – the Karoo's kangaroos – and striped polecats.

It's early morning and still dark as we set off on a game drive, snugly wrapped in fleecy ponchos. Our open 4x4 vehicle growls its way up a road cut precariously into the hillside. Kudus bound out of our path. We crest the hill as the sun peers over the highest peaks. Nearby, a giraffe duo gawks curiously at our intrusion.

Emerging from the vehicle, we make our way past the ruins of an early settler farmstead, and stop to photograph herds of eland, several small families of mountain zebras and the breathtaking views that unfold in every direction.

Winding down into a small valley, we come across a tiny graveyard and memorial to 11 British soldiers who lost their lives here during the Anglo-Boer War. Nearby is the sheep and goat kraal in which the skirmish took place, and the bullet holes in the roof of the shelter are as chilling today as they must have been more than 100 years ago. Special presentations about the Anglo-Boer War can be arranged for those who are interested in more detailed information.

Back at camp, we tuck into a hearty breakfast, then head to the library to read some more about this fascinating area. The library is extensive enough to keep most bibliophiles occupied for several days, and I while away a few hours lost in tales of history and bravery. I admire the comfort and attention to detail at this camp. We've been made to feel so welcome that I'd be happy to slip off my shoes and recline on a couch as though in my own home. Which is exactly how Iain (and the late Logie) would want us to feel.

details

When to go
Mount Camdeboo is open all year. Temperatures in winter (from May to July) can be low, with the possibility of snow on the surrounding mountains.

How to get there
The nearest town is Graaff-Reinet, about an hour away over good gravel roads. Port Elizabeth is the nearest city served by scheduled flights and is about three to four hours from the reserve by road. Charter flights may use the airstrips on neighbouring properties by prior arrangement.

Who to contact
Tel. (+27-49) 891 0570,
e-mail *reservations@mountcamdeboo.com*
or go to *www.mountcamdeboo.com*

mbotyi river
lodge

Wedged between a tumble of emerald hills and the pounding Indian Ocean,

Mbotyi is a tranquil refuge from the hurly-burly of city life.

It's a calm, clear morning as I hike along the lush green hills towards Shark's Point. Big waves crash onto the rocks below as we walk past two grazing cows before stopping on top of the cliffs for a breather. 'This is an awesome spot to see dolphins and whales,' says Mbotyi River Lodge manager, Sean Pike. 'Last week I saw a large pod just beyond the breakers.'

Situated at the mouth of the Mbotyi River ('place of beans' in the local Xhosa language) amidst a tumble of hills dotted with colourful thatched huts, Mbotyi Lodge is the perfect venue for a tranquil holiday. Accommodation is in 36 wooden cabins and 12 thatched bungalows, all with en-suite bathrooms, balconies and sea or lagoon views. The spacious grounds have a swimming pool, trampoline and children's playground. Meals are varied but, with the ocean on its doorstep, the lodge's speciality is seafood.

Outdoor lovers can choose from a range of activities, including 4x4 trails, mountain-biking, canoeing, bird-watching, fishing and horseriding. There are also many remote and beautiful beaches to explore. The area around the lodge is heavenly for hikers, with a multitude of trails, ranging from easy walks to challenging full-day hikes, to be enjoyed by both novice and experienced hikers. The routes go along beaches, past waterfalls, across cliffs and through unspoilt forests and rivers.

Birding in the area is spectacular, with regular sightings of the olive woodpecker, Knysna turaco, trumpeter hornbill

Magwa Falls is perfect for adrenalin junkies. I'm quite content to gaze at the spectacular torrents of water tumbling down sheer mossy cliffs

PREVIOUS SPREAD Mbotyi's wooden buildings blend sympathetically with their surroundings.

THIS SPREAD The lounge and deck is surrounded by greenery, and there's even a resident cat.

The pool is perfect for a cooling plunge after a long hot walk on the beach.

Little can beat the sensation of horseback riding at the water's edge.

The bedrooms are furnished with wood, cane and warm-coloured fabrics.

Magwa Falls.

and wailing cisticola, among others. Another species that birders will be keen to tick off is the Critically Endangered Cape parrot, of which fewer than 500 remain in the wild.

After settling in, I sit down to lunch – a delicious seafood buffet of oysters, mussels, crayfish, calamari and butterfish fillets. Later, we drive to the top of a mountain to watch the sunset. The road is rough and the vehicle battles all the way to the summit, but the endless view is worth the effort.

The next morning I wake early and take a tour to some of the waterfalls in the area. As we drive along the dusty roads, Mbotyi begins to waken. Women wash clothes in the river while others carry big buckets of water on their heads. The men are already hard at work, tilling their fields of bean and corn. The first stop is Fraser Falls, where we look down to the verdant depths of the forest. We drive on past Magwa Tea Estate, where men and women are harvesting the tea, plucking the green leaves and stuffing them into big hessian sacks. Magwa Falls is perfect for adrenalin junkies. You can foofy-slide over the falls and brave South Africa's longest abseil of 140 metres. I'm quite content to gaze at the spectacular torrents of water tumbling down sheer mossy cliffs to the gorge below.

Mbotyi is a friendly village and the local people are happy to interact with tourists. After a swim in the warm Indian Ocean, I stroll along the beach and get chatting to Samson Ncane, who works as the local marine resource catch monitor. 'My job is to measure the fish that people catch. If it is undersized, I teach them that the fish should be returned to the ocean. I was born in Mbotyi and it is a good place to live. There is much wood for fire, plenty of fish in the ocean and many cows that provide milk and help prepare the fields for our crops. Although we are poor people, we have everything we need,' he smiles.

details

When to go
Hiking is best in winter when the temperature is cool and conditions are mild. Summer can be very hot. Dolphins are a frequent sight off this coast, especially during the annual sardine run, which occurs in winter.

How to get there
From Umtata, take the R61 towards Port St Johns. Turn left at the signpost to Lusikisiki. After 41 kilometres, turn right at the signpost to Mbotyi. The lodge is at the end of this 26-kilometre-long road.

Who to contact
Tel. (+27-39) 253 7200/1, (+27-82) 764 1064/804 5142, e-mail *parthabs@pondoland.co.za* or *mbotyi@pondoland.co.za*, or go to *www.mbotyi.co.za*

eastern cape

Supertubes, Jeffreys Bay.

THE EASTERN CAPE is a playground of Big Five game reserves, rugged wild coastline and fascinating Karoo landscapes. This is the perfect destination when visiting with young children, as it is malaria free. From Port Elizabeth, head towards the Addo Elephant National Park to stay in one of the nearby private reserve lodges.

Then drive inland to experience the vast and fascinating thirstland of the Camdeboo region near Graaff-Reinet in the Great Karoo.

Back on the coast, don't miss the massive dunefields near Alexandria and the pristine coastline as you head north towards Nelson Mandela's birthplace on the Wild Coast.

For itinerary suggestions, contact:
AFRICA GEOGRAPHIC TRAVEL
Tel. (+27-21) 762 2180
E-mail *travel@africageographic.com*
Website *www.africageographictravel.com*

Port Elizabeth

South Africa's second-oldest city, Port Elizabeth is the commercial capital of the Eastern Cape and, with the towns of Uitenhage and Despatch, forms part of the Nelson Mandela Bay Metropole.

Its attractions are many, and include good weather, beautiful beaches (such as those at St Georges and Humewood), whale-watching, hikes and trails, museums, interesting settler architecture (the town was founded in 1799) and a casino. The rolling hills beyond Port Elizabeth shelter numerous wildlife reserves, with lions, crocodiles, giraffes, zebras, wildebeest, white rhinos, waterbuck, impala, reedbuck, warthogs and a wealth of birds. Many offer accommodation, while some are open for day visitors only and have restaurant facilities.

Addo Elephant National Park

The park was created in 1931 to protect a small group of elephants – the survivors of a once-enormous population that was virtually exterminated by trophy hunters, poachers and farmers. Today this finely tuned ecosystem is sanctuary to more than 450 elephants, as well as African buffaloes, black rhinos, a variety of antelope species and the unique flightless dung beetle, found almost exclusively in Addo. There are plans to expand the 164 000-hectare park into a 360 000-hectare megapark, which

Xhosa homestead.

ROGER DE LA HARPE

will include a 120 000-hectare marine reserve, within which are islands that are home to the world's largest breeding populations of Cape gannets and second-largest breeding population of African penguins. The park has a restaurant and a well-stocked curio shop.

Grahamstown

Also known as Settler City and the City of the Saints, due to its number of churches, Grahamstown is one of the oldest settlements in South Africa. It's home to a university, and bustles with students during term time. Visit the Albany Museum Complex to investigate local history, examine the Victorian camera obscura, admire the charming settler and Victorian architecture and read about the fascinating coelacanth fish. For those keen on local culture, visit the local township under the auspices of the Kwam eMakana project, which offers an authentic township experience, including a visit to a tavern and an overnight stay.

Graaff-Reinet

This charming town is called the 'Gem of the Karoo' and it appears as a bright oasis in the surrounding stark Karoo landscape. The town has more national monuments than any other in South Africa, and there's an interesting museum complex that documents its 220-year-old history.

Nearby is the Karoo Nature Reserve, popular with hikers, photographers and fans of flora and fauna. Within the reserve's boundaries is the Valley of Desolation, a moonscape of desolate beauty, where some 9 000 plant species have adapted to the harsh conditions. Paragliders can often be seen floating on the thermals with the Verreaux's eagles that nest in the rocky crags. North of the town is Nieu-Bethesda, and the home of the eccentric artist Helen Martins, who decorated her mystic sculptures and Owl House with crushed glass.

Jeffreys Bay

Each year, between May and August, low-pressure systems roll around the Cape St Francis headlands, generating huge swells that have earned Jeffreys Bay a reputation as one of the best surfing areas in the world. It is also known for the ornaments and curios made by local residents from the shells that are washed ashore. There's a small nature reserve in the town, and a host of coffee shops, restaurants and places to relax in the sun.

Wild Coast

This vast stretch of undulating hills, lush forest, spectacular beaches and churning waters is one of South Africa's most unspoilt areas. Reaching some 250 kilometres from the Kei River in the south to the Mtamvuna, the Wild Coast is a haven for hiking, horse

Sculptures by Helen Martins at the Owl House.

MARY DUNCAN

trails, game watching, cliff-jumping, abseiling, quad-biking, mountain-biking, fishing, canoeing, surfing, boat-based dolphin-watching and other watersports. There's not much in the way of game, but birdwatchers will enjoy ticking the 320 listed species. The area is also home to former South African President Nelson Mandela. Tourists can visit his birthplace at Qunu and get a glimpse into his life at the Nelson Mandela Museum in the same area.

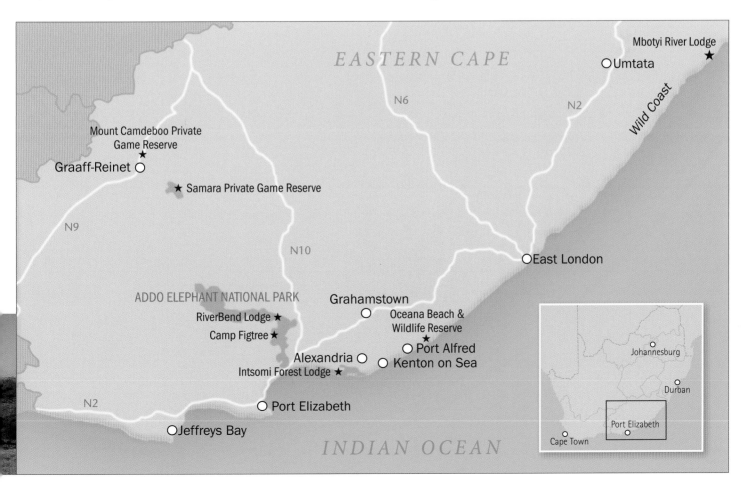

kingdom of the
kwazulu-natal

zulu

AmaKhosi Safari Lodge game drive.

There are three distinct regions in this province on South Africa's north-eastern coast. The southern part, including the culturally rich capital of Durban, has beautiful beaches that are popular with holidaymakers. Inland are rolling farmlands that culminate in the fortress of the Drakensberg mountains, with their towering peaks, rock art and wildlife reserves. To the north, the rich tropical region of Zululand is home to hippos and crocodiles and vast wetland parks.

lynton
hall

This award-winning lodge offers legendary cuisine, rambling, bird-filled gardens and five-star luxury.

I **missed lunch today.** It may have been a blessing in disguise, because the feast that awaits me definitely requires a healthy appetite. After pre-dinner drinks on the veranda, we take our places at the candlelit table, elegantly set with sparkling cutlery for the seven-course dinner.

Fine cuisine is the focal point of a stay at Lynton Hall. My mouth starts to water as I peruse the menu. First I'm served prawns with sweet chilli mayonnaise, followed by tasty asparagus soup with salmon ice cream. The duck-breast salad and beef carpaccio with Japanese curry yoghurt and goat cheese are both delicious, as is the main course of pork fillet with pickled vegetables. I'm glad I left some room for dessert, because the only description for the plate of assorted chocolate treats is ambrosial.

It's a bright, sunny day as I drive along KwaZulu-Natal's South Coast. I'm heading for Lynton Hall, one of South Africa's top five-star boutique hotels, located just 45 minutes south of Durban.

Entering the spacious grounds, a sense of calm washes over me, and I'm warmly welcomed at reception by Reyem Meyer. 'You are guaranteed to have a tranquil time here,' he smiles. 'We are known for our relaxing atmosphere, fine food and wonderful wines. We also have one of the most exotic gardens in the country and our plants include several rare species. Many guests just want to walk in our grounds and get away from it all.'

Built in 1895, Lynton Hall is set in 200 hectares of coastal forest. Its grounds include a tennis court and swimming pool, over 185 bird species and more than 100 recorded species of butterflies. The Garden Pavilion incorporates the Hall's new conference centre, an ideal venue for small conferences and weddings.

Accommodation is in 11 luxury suites, all with air-conditioning, en-suite bathrooms, underfloor heating

Fine cuisine is the focal point of a stay at Lynton Hall. My mouth starts to water as I peruse the menu

and satellite television. Massage treatments are available in the privacy of your room.

There are plenty of activities and sightseeing options for visitors, with the famous game reserves, beaches and mountains of KwaZulu-Natal all within easy reach. You can fish, sail, surf, take nature walks, visit arts and crafts shops or go scuba diving. The warm Indian Ocean is just 10 minutes away, with good swimming at Pennington Beach. Aliwal Shoal is famous for its corals and underwater life.

Mtamvuma and Oribi Gorge reserves have abundant birdlife, rare fauna and flora and ancient rock engravings. There are 21 superb golf courses within an hour's drive. The hotel also has its own 470-metre driving range, target greens, practice bunkers and a putting green.

On my final day I wake early and laze in bed, watching the palm trees rustle in the breeze outside my window. I stroll around the gardens, then relax at the pool with a good book before my final Lynton Hall lunch.

Yet again, it is a meal to remember. I start with chicken galantine with carrot purée and a salad of red lettuce and rocket. For the main course, I choose slices of springbok accompanied by cigars of mashed potato, vegetable shavings and star-anise *jus*. Later, on my way back to Durban, I'm already planning a return visit and more gastronomic pleasures.

PREVIOUS SPREAD The Lewis suite, one of Lynton Hall's 11 individually decorated luxury accommodation options.

This gracious property was built by the Reynolds family, who started a successful sugar mill in the area in the 1870s.

THIS SPREAD The manicured gardens invite guests to linger and stroll.

Every meal celebrates fine cuisine.

Conversation sparkles at the dinner table.

The lodge at night.

The Molly suite, named for the daughter of Frank Reynolds.

details

When to go
Lynton Hall is a year-round destination. Scuba divers may want to time their visit between June and November, when they can swim with ragged-tooth sharks. The annual sardine run occurs between June and August.

How to get there
The lodge is 45 minutes by road south of Durban.

Who to contact
Tel. (+27-39) 975 3122,
e-mail *info@lyntonhall.co.za*
or go to *www.lyntonhall.co.za*

leadwood
lodge

Unstressed animals, beautiful surroundings,
courteous service and mouthwatering cuisine are
the hallmarks of this secluded sanctuary.

Tala is a Zulu word meaning 'land of plenty', and these African plains are certainly home to a plethora of big game

PREVIOUS SPREAD Leadwood Lodge has been voted one of 'the coolest new hotels in the world'.

There's a heated pool for guests who enjoy a dip.

THIS SPREAD The furnishings are cosy, the colours warm and inviting,

The owner's motto of 'nothing straight, nothing painted' ensures an organic architectural style.

Hippos yawn and wallow in a dam.

The cuisine is based on the freshest produce, simply presented.

A romantic bedroom. The suites are completely private.

I wake early. It's still dark as my guide and I set off from Leadwood Lodge on a bush walk. Within minutes, we come across a large scattering of dung next to the path. 'A hippo has been here, and it's very fresh, probably just an hour old,' he says. We cut into the deep bush and my boots are soon soaked by the wet vegetation. I close my eyes and inhale the earthy smell.

Just ahead, a herd of zebras runs across the path and stops in the distance, stares at us and snorts a warning. We inspect different droppings and distinguish those of a giraffe, with acacia-leaf remnants inside them. A bush walk makes one appreciate the small things in nature; I would never have seen these details from the back of a vehicle.

The clouds disperse and a beautiful day beckons. Leadwood Lodge lies in Tala Private Game Reserve, a 3 000-hectare, malaria-free sanctuary set amongst the undulating hills of KwaZulu-Natal, just 45 minutes from Durban. Once home to cattle farms, the area was transformed into a wildlife sanctuary by Stuart Hilcove.

'I have always had a love of wildlife. Tala is a special place and I'm excited to share these beautiful surroundings with others. Also, to be playing a part in the conservation of our dwindling wildlife is an experience I shall always treasure,' he says.

Tala is a Zulu word meaning 'land of plenty', and these African plains are certainly home to a plethora of big game, including buffaloes, white rhinos, hippos, kudu, giraffes, zebras and rare species of buck such as oribi and sable antelope. The birdlife is also prolific – over 340 species having been sighted.

Leadwood Lodge was originally built by Hilcove as his dream home and was later converted into the luxury establishment it is today. Combining exceptional architecture and stunning interiors, the building is a creation of earth, water, glass and wood and designed on the ethic of 'nothing straight, nothing painted'.

Six secluded luxury cottages are romantically located in the bush and guarantee complete privacy. Each is tastefully finished with a high thatched roof and contains a wooden four-poster bed, a spacious lounge with a fireplace, indoor and outdoor showers and a large sundeck. The airy en-suite bathrooms are fitted with imported accessories. The main house includes a large lounge area with a central fireplace, a bar with a full-sized snooker table, a library, a heated infinity pool and a well-stocked wine cellar. The cuisine at Leadwood Lodge is another highlight and emphasis is placed on fresh produce, simply prepared and served as a five-course dinner. In 2004, Leadwood Lodge was voted by the US *Condé Nast Traveler* magazine as one of the 'coolest new hotels in the world'.

The main activities offered are game drives, bass fishing, birdwatching and guided bush walks. The game can also be viewed on horseback safaris, which are popular for those seeking a close encounter with the animals.

We set out on a late-afternoon game drive and come across a herd of giraffes. They are the most relaxed animals I've ever encountered, and continue grazing, totally unperturbed by our proximity. 'The animals at Tala are very relaxed because there are no major predators and this makes for good photographic opportunities,' says my guide, Richard Blackwood, as I click away in the warm afternoon light.

Later, as the sun drops, we stop at a dam. Scattered clouds are reflected in the water as we watch a pod of nine hippos. One honks at us and yawns, fearsomely displaying its huge, gaping jaws.

details

When to go
Tala Private Game Reserve is a year-round destination. Conditions in winter can be cold, but this is the ideal time to see animals as the vegetation is dry and sparse.

How to get there
From Durban, drive along the N3 towards Pietermaritzburg and take the Camperdown off-ramp. Turn left towards Umbumbulu Road and, after three kilometres, turn left at the T-junction. The entrance to Tala Reserve is 13 kilometres along this road.

Who to contact
Tel. (+27-31) 781 8000,
e-mail *info@tala.co.za*
or go to *www.tala.co.za*

rocktail bay
lodge

Turtles and other coastal delights combine with a sincere concern for responsible

tourism at this well-known getaway in the iSimangaliso National Park.

It's late afternoon and I'm travelling in a 4x4 along Maputaland's beach in search of nesting turtles. We find fresh tracks and stop to investigate. But we've arrived just too late. 'It was a loggerhead turtle and probably went back to the water just a few minutes ago,' says Mbongeni Myeni, my guide from Rocktail Bay Lodge.

Thousands of ghost crabs scuttle for safety as we cruise along the sand at the water's edge. Then, suddenly, we hit the jackpot. Telltale tracks lead to a loggerhead nesting at the back of the beach. She's already dug her body pit and excavated the chamber for her eggs. 'Once she starts laying she'll go into a trance and you'll be able to take photographs,' whispers Mbongeni.

I watch in wonder as the pearly white eggs drop softly into the sandy hole. After she's finished laying, the exhausted turtle uses her back flippers to cover the nest with sand. The tide is advancing, so reluctantly we leave her to her tiring task.

Rocktail Bay Lodge is located in the iSimangaliso (formerly the Greater St Lucia) Wetland Park, one of South Africa's World Heritage Sites. Named after a fishing trawler that was wrecked here during a cyclone in 1966, the lodge is situated in a coastal forest filled with animals, birds and plants.

Offshore is the Maputaland Marine Reserve, a coastal sanctuary with coral reefs that offer great snorkelling and scuba diving. Rocktail Bay is considered one of the top 10 dive sites in the world and the lodge has a fully accredited dive centre. Other activities include catch-and-release fishing, horseriding, guided walks and nature drives.

Rocktail Bay Lodge is owned and managed by Safari & Adventure Co., a company within Wilderness Safaris, a South African conservation organisation renowned internationally for its commitment to the environment and local communities. In keeping with these policies, guests can visit Gugulesizwe Cultural Village for an authentic Zulu experience that includes dancing and interactions with a traditional healer.

Accommodation is in 11 wooden chalets raised on stilts beneath the forest canopy. Each room has its own private deck, en-suite bathroom and outdoor shower. At the lodge's heart is a lounge and well-stocked wine cellar. A boardwalk winds through the dune forest to the beach.

The beaches around Rocktail Bay are host to scores of leatherback and loggerhead turtles that return to their place of birth to lay their eggs. A critically endangered species, leatherbacks are the largest turtles in the world and can grow to 1 000 kilograms. In Africa, their only nesting sites are in West Africa and here on the Maputaland coast.

Rocktail Bay's turtle research began in 1963 and is considered to be the longest ongoing scientific study of turtles in the world. The studies indicate that the local turtle population is one of the few in the world that is growing. Guests can adopt a turtle, with the funds going to the Maputaland Sea Turtle Research Project.

I join an excursion to Black Rock, where we hike along the cliffs and admire the view along kilometres of pristine beach. A lone fisherman stands on the shore, casting his line into the surf. After lunch, I join a small group for an outing to Hippo Pools, where a pod of 12 hippos has set up home in an inland dam.

The following morning I wake early and stroll along the walkway to the beach. Nobody is around and I amble along the shore, inspecting the life in the tidal rock pools. The sun rises, giving the foam a pink glint as the tide recedes. I put down my camera and plunge into the Indian Ocean's breakers.

PREVIOUS SPREAD A magical bedroom in the treetops.

The Rocktail Bay coastline is unspoilt and secluded.

THIS SPREAD A knowledgeable guide is an asset on a nature walk.

Every year, scores of leatherback and loggerhead turtles return to this coastline to lay their eggs.

Enjoy lunch beneath the patchwork shade of a spreading Natal mahogany tree.

You're ensured a good night's sleep in Rocktail Bay's cosy chalets.

Searching for turtles.

I watch in wonder
as the pearly white
eggs drop softly into
the sandy hole

details

When to go
Diving takes place all year, with better visibility from
September to May. Summer is the best time to see
nesting turtles. Turtle hatchlings are best observed
from the end of December to mid-March. Humpback
and southern right whales visit between June and
late August.

How to get there
The easiest way to get to Rocktail Bay Lodge is by
air. Guests are met at the airstrip. Those arriving by
road are given detailed directions when making their
reservation.

Who to contact
Tel. (+27-11) 257 5111,
e-mail *enquiry@safariadventure.co.za*
or go to *www.safariadventurecompany.com*

amakhosi
safari lodge

A paradise for creatures great and small, this luxurious retreat is managed by a frog-lover whose passion for the local environment will have you returning time and again.

Standing knee deep in the muddy water, I close my eyes and listen to the amplified sounds of an amphibian chorus

MARTIN HARVEY

Night has fallen and the still air is filled with high-pitched beeps and a myriad other loud amphibian calls. 'That's the bubbling kassina, one of the 32 species I've identified here,' says Alwyn Wentzel, frog fundi and manager of AmaKhosi Safari Lodge. 'We also hear golden leaf-folding frogs, sharp-nosed grass frogs and snoring puddle frogs.'

Under a star-filled sky, we don wellington boots and headlamps and wade into a shallow rain pan. My boots stick in the mud as I squelch over to where Alwyn is illuminating a painted reed frog clinging to the reeds. 'Most frogs are very colourful and pretty, but I am fascinated by their lifestyles. They can only breed and be active in the rainy season, so these frog safaris are seasonal,' he says, pointing out a white ball of foam where a frog has laid her eggs. Standing knee deep in the muddy water, I close my eyes and listen to the amplified sounds of an amphibian chorus.

AmaKhosi Safari Lodge is situated on the banks of the Mkuze River, in the 12 000-hectare AmaZulu Private Game Reserve in northern KwaZulu-Natal. The lodge (its Zulu name means 'a place of kings') consists of eight luxurious river suites, designed with a strong Zulu influence. Each suite contains a lounge, bedroom, stylish bathroom and private viewing deck overlooking the river.

There are also two deluxe honeymoon suites with open-plan interiors and plunge pools.

Other facilities include a swimming pool, library, curio shop and spacious lounge decorated with African artefacts and wooden furniture. Massage treatments are available on the pool deck, in the lush garden or in the privacy of your suite.

Game-viewing here is excellent, with regular sightings of the Big Five, either on game drives or guided walks. Cheetahs are also prolific in the area and birders will be in their element, with more than 400 species having been sighted.

'This is Big Five country, but what's really special about the region is the Mkuze River, which is the lifeline for the St Lucia Wetland area,' says Alwyn. 'It's important that the land alongside the river is protected, and in that sense we are helping to conserve the greater wilderness region of KwaZulu-Natal.'

Frogging safaris are an unusual highlight at the lodge, and were initiated by Alwyn. He has also launched micro-safaris that concentrate on insects and nature's smaller creatures.

After high tea, I set off for an afternoon game drive. Animals are everywhere and we spot herds of zebra, giraffe and wildebeest. We soon come across a big bull elephant that is heavily in musth. 'In this state all they want to do is mate and they can be very aggressive, so we won't follow him,' says Alwyn. We find a more relaxed individual grazing in an open field and watch as it happily munches away just metres from our vehicle.

The sun is about to set when we find a cheetah snoozing in the grass. He stirs lazily and stares at us, his spotted coat glowing in the lingering orange light. Our final sighting is of two male lions. 'There are so many animals around today, it's almost like a zoo,' Alwyn jokes.

The following morning we start our game drive just as the sun rises to reveal a cloudless sky. The highlight of the drive is an entertaining hour spent watching a breeding herd of elephants as they splash and drink in a muddy dam. The two-week-old baby slips and slurps, watching its mother and picking up tips on how to use its trunk.

Dinner tonight is served outdoors at the pool deck. But, before sitting down to eat, we're escorted to the kraal and are treated to traditional dancing and a lively drum display by the local Zulu community.

Later, I retire to the comfort of my suite and drift off to dreamland, lulls by croaks and harrumphs from the African bush.

PREVIOUS SPREAD The air-conditioned suites have en-suite bathrooms, a Jacuzzi, mini fridges and king-sized beds.

Exploring the grassy banks of the mighty Mkuze River.

THIS SPREAD A painted reed frog.

An elephant lumbers across the AmaKhosi parkland.

A cheetah snoozes in the grass.

Lush vegetation surrounds the pool.

Rich African colours have been used in the main lounge and bar.

details

When to go
Frogging safaris take place in summer, from November to March, which is also the best time for the micro-safaris. Wildlife viewing is good throughout the year, but bigger concentrations of game are visible in the dry, cooler months from April to October.

How to get there
There is an hour-long charter flight from Johannesburg to the lodge. By road, it is a five- to six-hour drive from Johannesburg, and four hours from Durban.

Who to contact
Tel. (+27-34) 414 1157, e-mail *info@amakhosi.com* or go to *www.amakhosi.com*

pakamisa
private game reserve

Cool breezes, dramatic scenery and a host of wild animals can be experienced by guests at Pakamisa from a unique perspective – the back of a horse.

PREVIOUS SPREAD Giraffes flourish in the lush Pakamisa terrain.

The setting sun casts a golden glow over Pakamisa and
its magical hills and valleys.

THIS SPREAD The swimming pool offers a view that
goes on forever.

Horseback safaris ensure an intimate encounter with the wildlife.

The suites are generously proportioned, with elegant furniture
and a roomy bed.

Zebras are seen regularly.

The lounge, furnished in rattan and other natural materials,
invites guests to rest a while and share their day's experiences.

PAKAMISA

It's a steamy summer day as I cruise along the N2 highway, heading for the peaceful paradise of Pakamisa Private Game Reserve. After passing fields of sugarcane, I ascend a mountain road and arrive at the lodge where owner Isabella von Stepski is waiting to meet me. 'Welcome to Pakamisa,' she smiles. 'This is a very tranquil place, and you'll love our panoramic views. But the highlight is definitely our horse safaris,' she tells me. They offer a unique way to view wildlife as guests are able to get up really close to wildebeest, warthog, kudu, impala, zebra and giraffe. 'You will see, it's an incredible experience,' she adds.

I've never been much of a horserider, my previous equestrian encounter being a rather saddle-sore adventure many years ago. But here, on the green plains of Pakamisa, I cast aside the painful memories and boldly swing into the saddle of my white Arabian horse. The sun is still low on the horizon as I set off with the safari group into the bush. Soon we're trotting beside several browsing giraffes. We also encounter zebra, warthog and a herd of inquisitive impala.

We amble slowly down a dirt road to the muddy edge of a dam where the horses stop to quench their thirst. My mount, Zulu, is intent on a swim and wades into the water before I can dismount. Much to the mirth of my fellow guests, Zulu rolls over, dunking both me and my camera equipment. I'm soaked, but luckily no serious damage is done to my Canon.

Pakamisa, which means 'to lift up', is spectacularly positioned in the mountainous region of northern Zululand. Its location on a plateau of the Pakamisa Mountain offers breathtaking views over the wide valley and plains. And it's so peaceful. Access to the lodge and its 2 500-hectare, malaria-free bushveld wilderness is restricted and guests can enjoy the experience without seeing other vehicles.

Isabella comes from a noble Austrian family and ensures that visitors are treated to her country's famed tradition of first-class hospitality. Just 16 guests are accommodated at a time in eight spacious suites, each with an elegantly finished bedroom, lounge and bathroom. Each suite reflects an African animal, a theme that is picked up in paintings and local artefacts. The main house includes a living room, library, bar and pool area. There's elegant dining to be had at El Prado restaurant. Meals are of international standards and often feature European cuisine and game specialities. Dinner on my first night is chilled cucumber soup, followed by roast lamb served with green beans and lemon-infused couscous. Dessert is coffee-flavoured crème caramel. All of it is delicious.

Activities at Pakamisa include archery, clay-target shooting, game drives and guided walks. Guests can expect to see many species of wildlife and the birdlife is prolific, with more than 200 species having been recorded. In addition, there are several day excursions to enjoy, including an outing to experience Zulu dancing and see local arts and crafts in traditional villages. Also popular is the conducted tour of the famous battlefields of the Anglo-Boer war. Fishing expeditions can be arranged to Jozini Dam and boat cruises through the renowned wetlands of iSimangaliso Wetland Park are offered.

After lunch and a swim, I take an afternoon game drive and am rewarded with sightings of zebras, giraffes and numerous other creatures. Sundowners are served on a mountain top, with gin and tonics and biltong snacks. The sun sinks, flushing the scattered clouds with pink and casting a glow over the Pakamisa plains.

I cast aside the painful memories and boldly swing into the saddle of my white Arabian horse

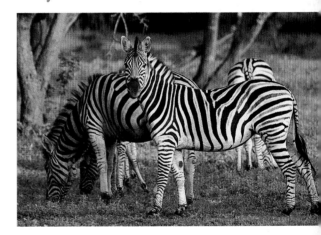

details

When to go
Summers can be hot, so the best time for horseback safaris is the cooler period between April and October.

How to get there
Pakamisa is situated 15 kilometres south-west of Pongola. You can fly from Johannesburg to Pongola Airport, where guests are met and transported to the lodge. Travelling by road from Johannesburg or Durban, you arrive at Pongola and follow the R66 towards Magudu until you see the Pakamisa sign. Turn right onto a dirt road. After a further eight kilometres, turn left to reach the entrance gate.

Who to contact
Tel. (+27-34) 413 3559,
e-mail *pakamisa@pakamisa.co.za*
or go to *www.pakamisa.co.za*

white elephant
safari lodge

Commune with elephants and rhinos, test your

tigerfishing skills or simply enjoy the elegant facilities at

this five-star lodge in the Pongola Game Reserve.

The silvery waters of Lake Jozini shimmer in the distance as I drive along the dirt road in Pongola Game Reserve. Impala bound off the path into the bushes, then stop and stare at me suspiciously.

A few kilometres further on, I arrive at the entrance to White Elephant Safari Lodge. Manager Phillip Wessels greets me with a lavender-scented face towel and homemade iced tea, both a welcome relief on such a steamy day. 'You're here to relax, so leave everything to me,' he says.

The lodge is located in the Pongola Game Reserve in northern Zululand and overlooks the western escarpment of the Lebombo Mountains and Lake Jozini. Proclaimed in 1894, the reserve was Africa's first, but disease and the outbreak of the Anglo-Boer War forced it to close soon afterwards. During the decades that followed, the animals were mercilessly hunted and the area was converted into cattle farms.

In 1954, conservationist Kallie Kohrs bought land here and, 40 years later, the area was re-established as a game reserve. Kallie's son, veterinarian Heinz Kohrs, re-introduced elephants in 1997, exactly 100 years after they were last sighted in the area. Today, Pongola is a sanctuary for a large variety of wildlife, including elephants, giraffes, wildebeest, zebras, hyaenas, buffaloes, rhinos and leopards. Birdlife is prolific, with over 350 species recorded.

Originally built in 1920, White Elephant Safari Lodge encapsulates the history and romance of the colonial era.

'When I was young, I used to dream that elephants were walking freely here. Now my dreams have become a reality'

Its eight luxurious safari-style tents, set in tranquil surroundings, each have an en-suite bathroom, outdoor shower and private veranda.

Activities include game drives, guided walks, canoeing, tigerfishing and sunset cruises. Cultural outings can also be arranged to Zulu villages. However, the highlights are the black rhino and elephant adventures. 'Through our elephant programme, guests have the opportunity to learn about each individual elephant, its history and its behaviour,' says Phillip. 'We also have a black rhino expansion project, supported by the World Wildlife Fund.'

I've arrived on an interesting day as an injured black rhino is about to be darted. 'Usually we wouldn't intervene, but black rhinos are highly endangered, so Ezemvelo KZN Wildlife gave their approval for us to help this animal,' explains Heinz, preparing the dart gun and tranquilliser. The rhino is immobilised and the team moves in to treat the wound sustained in a fight with another rhino. A few minutes later, the rhino struggles to its feet and staggers off into the bush.

Later, we head to Lake Jozini for a sunset cruise and have good sightings of hippo, crocodile, kudu, zebra and blue wildebeest. The birdlife is plentiful and we see saddle-billed storks, African fish-eagles, goliath herons and many others.

On the way back to the lodge we come across Ngani, Pongola Reserve's largest bull elephant, and we walk to within just 40 metres of the placid animal. 'When I was young, I used to dream that elephants were walking freely here,' says Heinz. 'Now my dreams have become a reality, and it's a privilege to share them with other people.'

I head for dinner – warthog sirloin served with mustard sauce, roasted potatoes and vegetables. I had no idea that such an unprepossessing animal could taste so delicious.

details

When to go
White Elephant Safari Lodge is open all year. The summer months can be extremely hot and humid; the best time to visit is in the cooler period between April to October.

How to get there
Flights are available from the major South African centres to Mkuze Airport, where guests are met and transferred to the lodge. The lodge is situated near the N2 highway, between Mkuze and Pongola. From Durban it is a four-hour drive; five from Johannesburg.

Who to contact
Tel. (+27-34) 413 2489,
e-mail *info@whiteelephant.co.za*
or go to *www.whiteelephant.co.za*

kwazulu-natal

Durban

The province's capital, Durban is South Africa's third-largest city and Africa's busiest port. It is famous for its wonderful climate, holiday attractions, subtropical landscapes, laid-back beach culture and watersports. Explore the Golden Mile, fascinating cultures, Art Deco architecture, food and craft markets and vibrant nightlife. For nature-lovers, there are numerous reserves and trails.

Drakensberg

This 200-kilometre-long mountain range, also known in the Zulu language as *uKhahlamba* (barrier of spears), is a lush World Heritage Site, with numerous wildlife parks and reserves, waterfalls, wilderness trails, rock-art sites and places to stay.

Midlands

Fertile farmlands straddle the region between the foothills of the Drakensberg range and the Indian Ocean coast. Numerous rivers cross the undulating plain, passing indigenous forests and small picturesque towns. A popular attraction is the Midlands Meander, an 80-kilometre arts-and-crafts route with more than 160 places of interest to visit, from restaurants to studios and outlets for weavers, potters, woodcrafters, leatherworkers, artists, metalworkers, box makers, herb growers, cheesemakers, beer brewers and many others. The midlands area was once the centre of military clashes of the Anglo-Boer War. Special tours can be arranged to visit the Battlefields Route.

Hibiscus Coast

South of Durban is a 70-kilometre-long stretch of coastline that attracts thousands of holiday-makers every year. At its core are the pretty vacation towns of Hibberdene, Port Shepstone, Shelly Beach, Margate, Southbroom and Port Edward. There's lots to do, from strolls along the beach to watersports, great restaurants, gracious living and a number of wildlife sanctuaries, including Oribi Gorge and Vernon Crookes nature reserves.

Horseback riding.

The Amphitheatre, Drakensberg mountains.

STEPHEN PRYKE

Sardine run & whales

Every year in June and July, millions of sardines migrate up the KwaZulu-Natal coast in a northerly direction in one of the most important biological occurrences in these waters. Approximately 23 000 dolphins, 100 000 Cape gannets, and thousands of sharks and game fish follow the shoals northwards, providing anglers with a bountiful harvest. Occasionally shoals come close inshore and can be netted from the beach. Whales (mainly humpback, occasionally southern right) are usually seen off the KwaZulu-Natal coast from July to November.

Hluhluwe-Imfolozi Park

The area north of Durban is rich in wildlife. Among its many sanctuaries is the 96 000-hectare Hluhluwe-Imfolozi Park, renowned for its

Rocktail Bay.

JEREMY JOWELL (2)

Cosmos.

DAVID ROGERS

rich diversity of animals, birds, trees and plant communities. It is the only park under formal conservation in KwaZulu-Natal at which the Big Five occur, and its white rhino conservation programme is world renowned. Facilities include self-guided walks and game drives, viewing hides, camps and picnic sites.

iSimangaliso Wetland Park

Previously known as the Greater St Lucia Wetland Park, this area on the northern KwaZulu-Natal coast was declared a World Heritage Site in 1999. The park's unique mosaic of ecosystems, ranging from swamps, lakes, beaches, coral reefs, wetlands, woodlands, coastal forests and grasslands, support an astounding diversity of animal, bird and marine life.

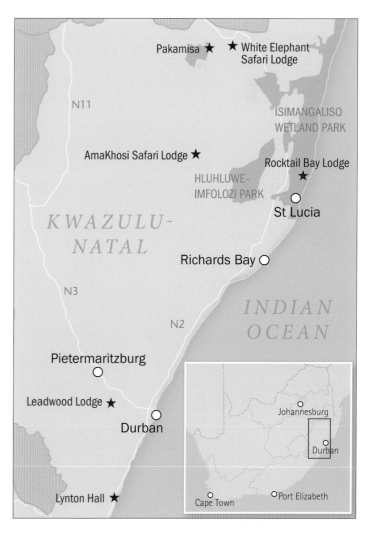

north by north-west

gauteng, limpopo & north west

Bush dinner at Morukuru Lodge.
IAN JOHNSON (5)

The wide bushveld plains of the northern reaches of South Africa were home to early hominids some three million years ago. Man is still very much in evidence here, especially in the vibrant cities of Johannesburg and Pretoria, which offer many attractions for visitors. To the north and west, vast game parks and private reserves focus their attention on restoring the landscape's natural wildlife.

rovos rail

Timeless and tranquil, travelling through the African veld by train is a singular experience. And there's one company that does it very well.

ROVOS RAIL

With a gentle jerk, the train starts to move out of Cape Town Station on its journey into the vast interior of South Africa. Table Mountain fades into the background as we clack along the tracks and very soon I'm accustomed to the rolling rhythm.

I relax in the lounge, sipping a gin and tonic, until the gong chimes for lunch. Sun streams in through the windows of the dining car as we sit down to starters of melon, mint and feta salad, followed by grilled salmon served with creamed potatoes, asparagus, vegetables and a herb-butter sauce. The meal is accompanied by a selection of the best South African wines. Dessert is a delicious cinnamon-dusted milk tart.

My hunger satisfied, I head for the open-air observation car and admire the Cape landscape. Large mountains loom in the distance as we pass undulating fields and green vineyards of the winelands. The locals smile and wave as we flash past their small villages.

Since its establishment in 1989, Rovos Rail has earned an international reputation as a five-star travel experience combined with an atmosphere of elegance and Victorian grandeur. The trains are considered to be the most luxurious in the world and carry a maximum of 72 passengers.

'Taking a journey on Rovos Rail is like being in a time warp,' says Rohan Vos, who initially started the railway as a home on wheels for his family. 'We've tried to combine the romance of train travel with accommodation, cuisine and service of the highest standard.'

Table Mountain fades into the background as we clack along the tracks and very soon I'm accustomed to the rolling rhythm

'Travelling by train, you see the country the way it is,' adds marketing executive Heike Gerntholtz. 'But the train is like a grand old lady and she does rattle and shake a bit, so we stop overnight to ensure our guests get a good night's sleep.'

The 36 spacious sleeper coaches have been refurbished to combine modern comfort with wood panelling and period Edwardian features. Each air-conditioned suite accommodates two people, and has an en-suite bathroom with original fittings. Each of the Royal Suites has its own lounge and, in the bathroom, a Victorian-styled bath in addition to the shower.

Each Rovos Rail train has two 42-seater dining cars to accommodate the passengers comfortably in one sitting. There is also an observation car, with large windows and open-air balconies. In keeping with the spirit of travelling in a bygone era, there are no radios or television sets on board and cellphone uage is restricted to the sleeping compartments.

Rovos Rail offers a variety of trips through South Africa. The regular route is a two-night journey between Cape Town and Pretoria, stopping off en route at Matjiesfontein and Kimberley. The trip between Pretoria and Durban only takes place in summer and guests enjoy two game drives along the way. Golf safaris and other special trips to destinations as far away as Namibia, Victoria Falls and Dar es Salaam in Tanzania are also offered, and the company caters for private group charters and extended lunch and dinner excursions.

A few hours along the line, we stop at the station in Worcester. For me, unfortunately, this is the end of the trip. Tonight the train will journey on to Matjiesfontein and through the Karoo, stopping at Kimberley before eventually reaching Pretoria. Reluctantly I step down onto the platform and watch as the elegant carriages slowly trundle off into the distance.

PREVIOUS SPREAD The train snakes through the Western Cape mountains at Montagu Pass.

THIS SPREAD The Royal Suites each have a Victorian-styled bath.

Warm wood, gleaming silver, crystal and starched linen add to the elegance of the dining experience.

Conversation flows in the comfortable lounge car.

The suites may be reminiscent of the early days of train travel, but air-conditioning ensures thoroughly modern comfort for guests.

The Rovos Rail cuisine is of the highest standard.

details

When to go

Rovos Rail operates selected itineraries year round. There are twice-weekly departures between Pretoria and Cape Town (and vice versa), fortnightly departures from Pretoria to Victoria Falls and Durban, and seasonal one-night journeys between Cape Town and George.

How to get there

The train trips run in either direction between Cape Town and Pretoria. The headquarters of Rovos Rail is the historic Capital Park Station just north of Pretoria. In Cape Town, departures are from the company's offices at 1 Adderley Street.

Who to contact

Tel. (+27-12) 315 8242,
e-mail *reservations@rovos.co.za*
or go to *www.rovos.com*

ant's nest

& ant's hill

Horseback safaris allow visitors an unusually intimate view of the game at these 'home from home' lodges in the majestic Waterberg.

We ride into a clearing and find four white rhinos contentedly grazing. The little one and its mother are very curious

The summer day begins to cool down as I saddle up and swing onto the back of my mount, Limpopo. I'm visiting Ant's Hill, a luxury lodge in the Waterberg, and am about to embark on my first horseride for many years.

Limpopo sets a languid pace and I trot along, slowly becoming accustomed to the equine rhythm. 'A horseback safari is a wonderful way to watch wildlife,' says my guide Sam Malamela. 'It's much more exciting than viewing the animals from a 4x4 vehicle.'

Limpopo is a well-behaved horse and stands still when eland, kudu and a herd of zebras cross our path and bound away into the bushes. We ride into a clearing and find four white rhinos contentedly grazing. The little one and its mother are very curious and move towards us slowly. It's a special sight to witness these bulky animals from such close quarters and I click away with my camera continuously. The big-horned creature walks right up to us. My stomach tightens and a surge of adrenalin rushes through me. But Limpopo is used to these close encounters and remains calm. As the sun sinks, we leave the rhinos, and pass 15 giraffes ambling through a field, bathed in the last golden rays of light. It's time to head back. The horses, sensing that they are heading home for dinner, pick up the pace.

Ant's Nest and Ant's Hill are bush homesteads situated on adjoining private game reserves in the malaria-free Waterberg. Both lodges can be booked on an exclusive basis.

Hosted by Ant and Tessa Baber, Ant's Nest accommodates a maximum of 12 guests. The colonial-style house is filled with furniture made of local materials and colourful fabrics. Outside, there's a 15-metre heated swimming pool surrounded by sprawling lawns and indigenous plants.

Set apart from the main lodge, Ant's Hill was built on the edge of a cliff and has breathtaking views across the Waterberg. It also caters for 12 guests and consists of two secluded honeymoon suites, a bedroom for two located above the main lodge, and a family cottage.

There are over 40 species of game on the property, including rare sable antelope, giraffe, buffalo, blue wildebeest, eland, white rhino, and more than 300 species of birds. Nocturnal species sometimes spotted are caracal, aardvark, brown hyaena, porcupine, bat-eared fox and civet.

Activity-wise, the undoubted highlight is the horseback safaris. Those who prefer walking can go on guided bush walks, which offer an intimate insight into the flora and fauna.

Children of all ages can participate in the activities but there are also toys and games to keep them occupied. Guests can also relax at the pool or enjoy a massage. Excursions are offered to view Bushman paintings or the Rhino Museum, where you can hand-feed an orphaned rhino.

As I walk around the grounds, the rim-flow pool and its comfortable loungers catch my eye and I make a mental note of where to take my afternoon siesta. After a lunchtime bush barbecue, I laze away the afternoon, making the most of the glorious weather. The tranquil time of day arrives and we enjoy sundowners on the wooden deck looking out to a pink sunset over the distant hills.

Next morning I wake before dawn and set off for a bush walk through fields still glistening with dew. 'Look, rhino tracks, they passed through just an hour ago,' says my guide. A herd of blesbuck runs away as we approach, but the dominant male stands his ground and snorts out a warning.

We stop to photograph the circular web of a kite spider, backlit by the rising sun. Regretfully, I head back to the lodge to start packing my bags.

PREVIOUS SPREAD The thatched Ant's Nest homestead has a warm, African atmosphere.

THIS SPREAD Guests can enjoy a relaxing massage beside the pool.

Rhinos viewed from horseback.

A sunken bath and the sounds of the indigo night spell romance.

Meals are served on the wooden deck, with a magnificent view.

The bedrooms are furnished with local materials.

details

When to go
From November to March, the days can be very hot, with afternoon thunderstorms. Winters (June to August) are mild in the day with very cold mornings.

How to get there
Travelling from Johannesburg, take the N1 north. At the third tollgate (Kranskop), turn onto the R33 to Nylstroom (Modimolle). Proceed through Nylstroom to Vaalwater. Through the town, turn right towards Ellisras (Lephalale). After 11 kilometres, turn right on a gravel road to Dorset. The sign for Ant's Nest is 10 kilometres further on. Private road transfers or air charters can be arranged.

Who to contact
Tel. (+27-14) 755 3584, e-mail *reservations@waterberg.net* or go to *www.waterberg.net*

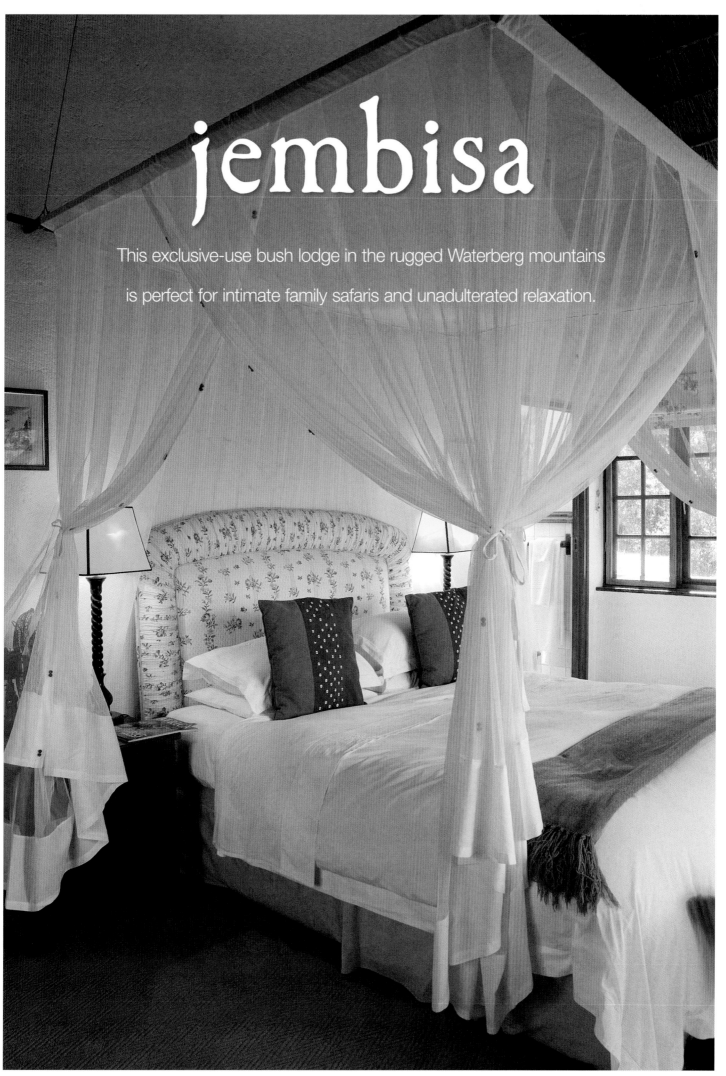

jembisa

This exclusive-use bush lodge in the rugged Waterberg mountains

is perfect for intimate family safaris and unadulterated relaxation.

A line of orange light cuts across the Limpopo horizon as dawn breaks in the Waterberg. I dress quickly, gather up my camera gear and set off with guide Steven Leonard for a hike down to the Palala River. As we walk through the bush, the sun rises, casting warm shafts of light through the green foliage. Steven points out the intricate web of a golden orb-web spider. Small grass-hoppers are trapped in the silk that is still glistening with droplets of dew.

Birds sing, monkeys chatter and a fine mist rises off the river. A lot of animals have walked here recently and we see tracks of giraffe, zebra, wildebeest, kudu, water-buck and Cape clawless otter. 'This flattened section of grass is where a hippo passed early this morning. The dung that it scattered is still very fresh,' says Steven. I close my eyes for a few moments and listen to the still-ness. The only sounds are the soft chirping of crickets and the melodic chorus of a host of birds. Then, after scouting the river for crocodiles, we take off our boots and wade across to where a lavish bush breakfast has been laid out by the Jembisa staff.

Situated in the Waterberg's malaria-free Palala River Reserve, Jembisa is a safari experience with a difference. Only one booking can be made at a time, ensuring that your stay is intimate and private. Jembisa is therefore the perfect place for families and small groups looking to experience the African safari on an exclusive basis.

The stone-and-thatch lodge, originally built as a fam-ily home, is beautifully designed, with spacious rooms decorated in an Afro-colonial style. There are five luxury en-suite bedrooms, three of which have private balconies. Bunk beds for children and cots for babies are available.

Certain activities have been designed especially for children, such as guided bush excursions, bug walks and slide shows. There are also children's books, games and a child-minding service.

Meals at Jembisa take place in a variety of settings, with bush picnics and dinners under the stars being very popular. Activities include game drives, bush walks and night excursions, on which you can see nocturnal animals such as brown hyaenas, aardvarks, civets and porcupines. Adventurous guests can spend a night camping in the wilderness. The reserve also has Bushman paintings and archaeological sites to explore. Alternatively, you may want to relax at the swimming pool, play tennis, go for cycling or enjoy a massage. Other activities in the vicinity are horseriding, elephant-back safaris, scenic helicopter flights and a visit to the Rhino Museum.

After a tasty lunch of chicken-breast fillets with peanut sauce, I relax at the pool, enjoying the warm sunshine. In the late afternoon we head out for a game drive and cross a bridge over the Palala River, where a pod of hippos glares up at us. We spot several species of animals – waterbuck, zebra, giraffe, warthog and blue wildebeest. But the highlight is the discovery of four white rhinos grazing in an open field. These inquisitive creatures have poor eyesight, but their sense of smell and hearing are finely tuned. The bulky beasts approach us and I step noiselessly out of the vehicle to lie flat on the ground for some eye-level photographs. One rhino, attracted by the click of my camera, moves in a little too close for comfort. A crescent moon hangs in the blue heavens and the sun sets in a blaze of gold as the rhinos head off to a waterhole, silhouetted against the darkening sky.

PREVIOUS SPREAD Dinners can be taken in the bush beneath a canopy of stars.

There are five luxury en-suite bedrooms.

THIS SPREAD The bush lodge was built as a family home, with spacious, airy rooms.

For many guests, the rhinos are the prime attraction.

A family game drive.

The lodge is finished with cool stone floors and Africa-themed furnishings.

Younger family members are especially important to the staff at Jembisa.

A crescent moon hangs in the blue heavens and the sun sets in a blaze of gold as the rhinos head off to the waterhole

details

When to go
Jembisa is open all year. The Waterberg area is hot in summer, while winters produce mild days with low temperatures at night and in the early morning.

How to get there
From Johannesburg, take the N1 highway north towards Polokwane. Turn off at the third toll gate to Nylstroom/Modimolle, then on to Vaalwater. Turn right towards Melkriver, proceed for 42 kilometres and turn left onto a gravel road to Melkriver School/Lapalala. After six kilometres, turn right at an old Cape Dutch farmhouse, pass the Rhino Museum – the main entrance to Jembisa Lodge lies three kilometres further along this road.

Who to contact
Tel. (+27-14) 755 4415, e-mail *info@jembisa.com* or go to *www.jembisa.com*

shibula lodge
& bush spa

Just two-and-a-half hours north of Johannesburg, this romantic

haven lies in an unspoilt, game-rich wilderness.

PREVIOUS SPREAD The dining room gleams with well-polished furniture, gentle lighting and local works of art.

Sundowners beneath an endless African sky.

THIS SPREAD Spend an hour or two on the pool deck.

Shibula is home to the Big Five.

Guests gather in the outdoor boma for a convivial barbecue.

Stalking a rhino.

Dream of wildlife and wide open spaces in the comfortable beds.

Driving through green fields, I spot animals that are gleaming and healthy, testament to the good rains that fell earlier this summer. As I enter Shibula Lodge and Bush Spa, the staff greet me with a welcoming song and manager Ulrich Schutte briefs me on a few safety points. 'We're an unfenced camp and are often visited by animals at night. Sometimes elephants drink from the pool and lions walk along the paths. We've also seen leopard and buffalo tracks, so you will always be escorted to and from your room after dark.'

Shibula is a five-star establishment in the Welgevonden Game Reserve in Limpopo Province. This 36 000-hectare malaria-free protected area contains the Big Five and is home to an extraordinary diversity of plant life and more than 350 species of birds.

The lodge is named after a female black rhino that grew up in Namibia before being incarcerated in a European zoo. Rescued by conservationists, the animal was brought back to Africa, where she was returned to the wild and became the first rhino to produce calves in these circumstances.

Voted as one of the top 10 romantic destinations in South Africa, the lodge also has a spa. Here, guests can pamper themselves with massage and beauty or body treatments. There is also a well-equipped gym, curio shop and a cellar stocked with an excellent selection of South African wines, hand-picked by Shibula's owner, Francois Klomp, who is the owner of Freedom Hill Wine Estate. Accommodation is in eight luxuriously furnished suites with indoor and outdoor showers, with deep, draped beds, Victorian-styled baths and private patios.

After lunch I swim and sunbathe at the rock-edged pool before joining a late-afternoon game drive. 'We'll head over to the plains where lions were sighted last night,' says the guide. The heat subsides as we bounce along the dusty road and, nearing a mud pool, we come across two white rhinos and a calf. A lioness and her three cubs watch warily in the background until one of the rhinos approaches and the little ones scamper for the safety of nearby bushes. We motor on towards a large herd of zebra and stop for sundowners. We sip our gin and tonics, watching the graceful ungulates amble amongst the trees in the soft dusk light. The red sun slips below the horizon and we drive in the dark, listening to the nocturnal chorus of croaking frogs and chirping crickets. But the overwhelming sound is the high-pitched stridulation of cicadas.

Dinner is a lantern-lit barbecue in the outdoor boma where we feast on roasted butternut and apple soup for starters, followed by grilled gemsbok fillet, served with a peanut and whisky sauce, pepperdew basmati rice and vegetables. Dessert is a delicious banana and toffee pie. I sleep deeply.

Next day, I wake to a crystal-clear dawn and set out on a game drive as the bush begins to waken. A call comes over the radio that the lions have just killed a zebra. We speed over to the waterhole and find the pride feeding voraciously. The three cubs, their muzzles stained red with blood, chomp away at the rear. 'With plenty of food and water, you can be sure they won't be moving much today,' smiles the guide.

The heat subsides as we bounce along the dusty road and ... we come across two white rhinos and a calf

details

When to go
Temperatures can get extremely high between November and March; in winter, conditions are mild during the day and chilly at night and on early-morning game drives.

How to get there
Take the N1 from Johannesburg north to Polokwane (Pietersburg). At the third tollgate, proceed along the R33 to Modimolle (Nylstroom). Go through the town and travel for 60 kilometres to Vaalwater. Continue straight for about 25 kilometres to reach Welgevonden's main gate. From here it's less than a kilometre to the lodge.

Who to contact
Tel. (+27-21) 882 8206,
e-mail *reservations@shibulalodge.co.za*
or go to *www.shibulalodge.co.za*

jaci's safari lodge
& jaci's tree lodge

A visit to these lodges, situated in the wildlife-rich Madikwe Game

Reserve on the edge of the Kalahari Desert, will almost guarantee

a sighting of African wild dogs and the impressive black rhino.

Watch out for the chef's mouthwatering kudu *potjie* – the meat has been soaked in red wine for four hours. It is delicious!

It is early morning, and there is a distinct chill in the autumn air as I board the safari vehicle. The driver is Deon de Villiers, the manager of Jaci's lodges, and our mission is to find two of Madikwe's endangered species – black rhino and African wild dog. We set off through the bush to an area favoured by black rhinos for its vegetation and lack of disturbance. The sun's rays are just starting to lighten the cloudy sky as we reach this 'rhino hotspot'. Ancient leadwood trees stand like skeletons, silhouetted eerily against the sky.

The radio suddenly crackles into life with the message that two lions are heading in our direction. We quickly move into position and wait. Increased bird calls alert us of the visitors. Then, from the bushes, we see the black mane of a huge male lion appear, followed by the blond head of his brother. They give our vehicle a quick glance, then silently pad past us.

We turn to follow them when Deon's sharp eyes identify the fresh tracks of a black rhino. Whispering, he informs me that the animal had passed over our tracks moments before we spotted the lions.

We decide to turn back to the lodge for breakfast, when the radio comes alive again with the word *makanyane*, wild dog in the Setswana language. A pack has been spotted at the entrance to Jaci's. We hurry back, only to discover that the dogs have chased a group of impala past the camp into a very dense area. However, we are greeted by six African wild dog statues that guard the entrance to the lodge.

The name Jaci's is synonymous with the huge, wildlife-rich-Madikwe Game Reserve, which lies on the edge of the Kalahari Desert, and with wild dogs. The dreamchild of Jan and Jaci van Heteren, Jaci's Safari Lodge was created in 2000 on the banks of the Groot Marico River. Two years later, they built Jaci's Tree Lodge in the dense riverine forest. Both lodges are strategically positioned close to an established and well-used waterhole, under a grove of tamboti trees.

The accommodation at both lodges is superb, with a real home-from-home appeal. The suites at Jaci's Safari Lodge have walls of stone and canvas, and a shaggy thatched roof that has authentic safari appeal. Inside, the furnishings are warm and welcoming. Jaci's Tree Lodge has eight stilted suites in the riverine forest, built at heights above the ground of up to five metres. Raised walkways link the suites with the main lodge, where meals are served, weather permitting, in the boma around an open fire beneath the stars. Watch out for the chef's mouthwatering and irresistible kudu *potjie* – the meat has been soaked in red wine for four hours. It is delicious!

For families, the separate Nare Suite and Safari Cottage are ideal. And, for those bent on maintaining their fitness, there is also a fully equipped gym situated between the lodges as well as a children's play area overlooking the river.

On the community front, I was delighted to hear from Simon 'Sticks' Bogatsu, the manager of Jaci's Tree Lodge, of the existence of a staff trust, which allows any member of staff who has been in the employ of the company for five years or more to own shares in Jaci's. Simon and 15 other staff members are shareholders, and reap the rewards of their hard work in the form of dividends.

PREVIOUS SPREAD Lion siblings, one dark-maned, the other light, pad through the bush.

An ancient leadwood tree is silhouetted in the evening light.

THIS SPREAD Preparing for dinner at Jaci's Tree Lodge boma.

The pool and deck area at Nare Suite overlook the private waterhole.

Unique design and quirky local artefacts decorate the main living area at Jaci's Safari Lodge.

The beautiful 'jungle shower' at Jaci's Tree Lodge.

A bedroom at Jaci's Tree Lodge.

details

When to go
Jaci's Safari Lodge and Jaci's Tree Lodge are open all year.

How to get there
Scheduled flights leave twice daily from Oliver Tambo International Airport direct to Jaci's lodges. Private charters can also be arranged on request. By road, the lodges are an easy four-hour journey from the airport. Visitors can drive themselves or arrange transport with the lodge.

Who to contact
Tel. (+27-14) 778 9900/9901, (+27-83) 700 2071 or 447 7929, e-mail jaci@madikwe.com or go to www.madikwe.com

mateya
safari lodge

Art and elegance combine with a plethora of wildlife at Mateya,

a lodge that pays homage to an intrepid African queen.

Its five thatched suites are so well hidden among the rocks that the view from each includes no glimpse of its neighbours

PREVIOUS SPREAD Kenyan artist Donald Greig's sculpture of a lioness chasing an impala stands in the lodge's entrance.

Lions are a 'must-see' on every safarigoer's wishlist.

THIS SPREAD A cool view across thornveld plains to distant hills.

In the tranquil suites, the linen is high-quality, the cushions are inviting and the vista is endless.

An elephant strolls by within full view of the lodge.

A young zebra.

Dinners are sometimes served at the wooden boma in front of the lodge.

Driving through the entrance of Mateya Safari Lodge, I was greeted royally, with big smiles and open arms. It was a fitting welcome to a lodge named after an African queen who, according to folklore, once journeyed south from her drought-stricken home to visit the legendary Rain Queen, Modjadji. En route, she set up camp in the area now known as Madikwe, in the North West Province. Modjadji did grant rain, they say, although Queen Mateya did not survive the journey home.

Years later, an American, Susan W. Mathis, also made a long journey to Africa and fell in love with its wide open spaces. Learning of the legend, she built her home and lodge in the same area in which the queen had camped, and named it Mateya in her memory. A bronze bust of this brave regent graces its entrance.

Soon after our arrival, the head guide, Philip Hattingh, called excitedly that wild dogs were hunting wildebeest in front of the lodge. Rushing to the huge front deck, we saw the tail end of a pack of dogs as the herd of wildebeest rallied to face their attackers, repelling them to the opposite side of the large waterhole in front of the lodge. It was an amazing and unexpectedly intimate first impression, and the adrenalin pumped through our veins.

Later, while walking to our suite, I noticed a leopard perched on one of the rocks. It's a bronze statue, created by well-known sculptor Donald Greig. The lodge's owners are dedicated collectors of African art, and their gallery of pieces from across the continent is displayed throughout the property. There are paintings by South African artists such as Paul Augustinus and Graham Kearney, sculptures by Dylan Lewis and Donald Greig, and historical artefacts such as Dogon stools, Yoruba fonts and Bambara marionettes from West Africa.

Mateya Lodge nestles between protective boulders in the Gabbro Hills in the centre of the 75 000-hectare Madikwe Game Reserve. Its five thatched suites are so well hidden among the rocks that the view from each includes no glimpse of its neighbours. From the cool interior of ours, the hand-crafted mahogany bed beckoned, with its fine linen and plush cushions. I looked around. There was a double shower (plus an outdoor one), a bath positioned so that one can watch the passing wildlife parade, a fireplace, a private plunge pool and various seating areas, all with endless views of the lodge's waterhole and across the thornveld plains to the shadowy Tweedepoort escarpment in the distance.

Mateya's menu is a fusion of African and European cuisine, and the staff are discreetly attentive. After an excellent lunch, we were ready to explore the reserve with Philip. Our game-viewing vehicle was one of the most well-equipped and comfortable that I have had the pleasure to be in and, scrambling aboard, we hoped to see a few of Madikwe's 'Super Seven' – leopard, lion, cheetah, elephant, buffalo, African wild dog and rhino. More than 350 bird species have been recorded. Our sightings far exceeded our expectations – male lions on an eland kill, female lions attempting to hunt impalas, a black rhino that lumbered into view as we sat watching lions at a zebra kill. Just when I thought it impossible to see anything else, we encountered a male leopard draped in a tree less than 60 metres from the entrance to the lodge.

That night, we snuggled down between the sheets and fell asleep, lulled by thoughts of beautiful animals and the inky African night.

details

When to go
Mateya Lodge is open all year.

How to get there
Madikwe Air Charter, in conjunction with Federal Air, has a daily one-hour shuttle flight from Johannesburg to Madikwe airstrip. A Madikwe representative meets guests for the 10-minute drive to the lodge.

Who to contact
Tel. (+27-14) 778 9200,
e-mail *info@mateyasafari.com*
or go to *www.mateyasafari.com*

molori

Molori beats with the pulse of Africa, from its diversity of

wildlife to the warmth of its décor and hospitality.

After landing at Molori's private helipad, I was welcomed with a smiled greeting and a chilled banana marula smoothie that slid down easily. I was led to my room, past beautiful pools that flowed one into the other, following the organic shape of the lodges structure. The air was still and tranquil, and I could feel a sense of peace seep into my muscles.

Molori is the Setswana word for a 'dreamer', and this beautiful lodge in the Madikwe Game Reserve is both the vision of its owners and an enticement for visitors to relax and put their cares behind them. Around the lodge are sundecks on which to unwind with a good book and a glass of chilled juice or wine, and gaze across the veld to the distant Dwarsberg.

My suite is warm and charmingly decorated with natural materials in shades of cream. Light infuses the rooms with a golden glow. Like the rest of the lodge, the décor is luxurious yet extremely comfortable.

While my bags are being unpacked by my personal butler, I head for the bar and listen to the other guests talking about the sightings of the day. I admire the double fireplace that separates the bar from the lounge, where a baby grand piano waits for a talented person to lift its lid. Folding glass walls disappear to make a seamless whole of the interior and outdoors, with striking views over the plains to the far hills.

I dine on a starter of sesame-seed-seared tuna and tempura vegetable salad, followed by a superb springbok loin. Molori's head chef is Willie Malherbe, who has extensive international experience. His cuisine focuses on the freshest produce, and ostrich and venison make regular appearances. During my

Around the lodge are sun-decks on which to unwind with a good book and a glass of chilled juice or wine

PREVIOUS SPREAD The turquoise pool twinkles in the light of Molori's evening lamps.

THIS SPREAD A zebra. Molori's wildlife can be seen on morning and evening game drives, and on nature walks.

Natural products – stone, cotton, wood and thatch – have been used throughout the lodge.

The cuisine appeals to both the eye and the taste-buds.

The sundecks are raised on stilts above the vegetation, allowing uninterrupted views of the veld.

A bushveld massage.

visit, fresh crayfish and prawns were on the menu. The breakfasts were incredible, with my favourite dish being truffle-infused scrambled eggs and smoked salmon.

The following morning, with a real desire to see the wildlife that Madikwe is famed for, I decide to take a walking safari. Greg Lederle, the general manager and a highly qualified guide, volunteers his services, and we take to the bush. Soon we come across fresh signs of a breeding herd of elephants, and Greg suggests we tread warily to avoid the cows, who tend to be overly protective. We hike onwards, with my informed guide stopping regularly to point out the little wonders that would be missed on a game drive – the caterpillars, the insects, spoor and dung tracks. I am completely captivated.

Feeling hunger pangs, we turn back to the lodge and, on the entrance road, meet a large bull elephant. 'That's Tsokwane,' Greg tells me. 'He came here from the Kruger National Park, and is the largest elephant in the reserve.'

Before dinner, I decide to take advantage of the spa. First I go for a steam, then have a deep-tissue massage to loosen the knots gained on my walk. I finish with a re-energising plunge in the chiller pool, and emerge feeling like a new man. For that real bushveld feeling, visitors can also have a healing and relaxing massage outdoors.

Later, after another delicious meal and a glass or two of red wine from Molori's substantial cellar, I visit the giant telescope on the property. I look from star to star, investigating the magical night sky. Then I return to my suite, sink into the deep mattress, and descend into dreamland.

A tranquil corner in one of the Presidential Suites.

Guests would be forgiven for finding it difficult to leave the comfort of their suites.

Dinner Molori-style, beneath the stars.

A private piece of heaven.

Walking tours are recommended for a really intimate view of nature.

We hike onwards, with my informed guide stopping regularly to point out the little wonders that would be missed on a game drive

details

When to go
Molori Safari Lodge and Spa is open all year.

How to get there
Most guests make use of Molori's private aircraft service to visit the lodge. However, Federal Air offers a 50-minute daily shuttle service from Oliver Tambo International Airport in Johannesburg to Madikwe Game Reserve's airstrip, from where transport can be arranged.

Who to contact
Tel. (+27-14) 778 9903 or (+27-82) 613 5723,
e-mail *info@molori.co.za*
or go to *www.molori.co.za*

morukuru
lodge

This private villa on the Marico River offers

home-from-home accommodation, safaris

to order and an unsullied bushveld setting.

It is late January – midsummer in the dry northern reaches of South Africa. This is when the afternoons produce sudden and violent storms, the thunderclaps reverberating across the hills. Here, in Madikwe Private Game Reserve, the ground has responded to the soaking, producing lush, green growth.

I am driving through this wildlife wonderland with Quintin van Vuuren, an ex-Zimbabwean guide who, assisted by his wife Lucy, is the manager of Morukuru Lodge. Accompanied by the tracker, Thomas Ubisi, we are heading towards the Marico River and this five-star luxury retreat.

Morukuru Lodge is the private home of Ed and Anke Zeeman, a Dutch couple who so love the wild African bushveld atmosphere that they built the homestead as their second home. At its entrance is one of the largest tamboti trees I have ever seen – *morukuru* is the Setswana word for this beautiful bushveld specimen.

As I enter the main building, I am greeted with an ice-cold lime and soda. I am immediately struck by the stylish, yet homely décor. Elegant wooden furniture is accented with fabrics in crisp red, fresh citrusy orange and lime green. This is the central living area, with a lounge filled with comfortable chairs, and I decide to return later to relax against the plump cushions with a good book. I am told that, when the winter nights draw in and the temperature plummets, the curtains are drawn and everyone chills out in front of the fireplace. I almost wish it were winter. There's also a dining-room with a table for 10, although dinner is often served on the pool deck or at the boma outside.

Overlooking the western Madikwe Reserve, we watch as the sun's final rays lower the light on our bush banquet

PREVIOUS SPREAD Nature's skyscrapers.

Alfresco dining on the tree-shaded deck.

THIS SPREAD Bushveld vegetation ensures privacy for guests who enjoy an outdoor bath.

Leo lolls in the long grass.

Outdoor dining at Morukuru is an elegant affair.

Floor-to-ceiling windows assure 24-hour views.

The staff are friendly and professional, and will even provide impromptu musical entertainment.

Apart from the lodge, Morukuru has a private, exclusive-use villa designed expressly for families and small, intimate groups. It has three elegant bedrooms, each with its own en-suite bathroom and private deck, and a family room with a huge sofa that folds out to form two super-sized single beds (there's room for six adults and four children). The family room's facilities include a television, DVD, Internet and satellite access. On one wall are intriguing, mushroom-shaped lights, which cast a warm glow.

The villa has its own staff that are discreetly attentive. During my brief stay, I was waited on by my personal butler, and had every dietary requirement satisfied by the excellent chef.

After high tea, including a moist honey-berry sponge cake, I am joined by Quintin, who has guaranteed I will see some of Madikwe's elephants on our afternoon drive. (Morukuru is situated on 2 500 hectares of private land adjoining the greater Madikwe Reserve.) We board the special game-viewing vehicle and soon encounter signs of fresh elephant activity. Within minutes we find a breeding herd of more than 30 elephants. Quintin explains that the pachyderms enjoy this part of the reserve because it is tranquil, with far less game-viewing activity than is common in other protected areas. There's lots of other wildlife here, too, including rhinos, cheetahs, zebras, African wild dogs, lions and giraffes. Birdlife is also abundant.

We stop for sundowners, and enjoy our gin and tonics to a backing track of evening birdsong and little else. We board the vehicle and start to head in what I think is the direction of the camp. Instead, Quintin has taken a different route to a bushy rise, where dinner awaits. We sit down and enjoy a wonderful meal in one of the most spectacular settings imaginable. Overlooking the western Madikwe Reserve, we watch as the sun's final rays lower the light on our bush banquet.

details

When to go
Morukuru is a year-round destination. Summers are hot, with afternoon thundershowers, and winters are cold and dry. Game-viewing is best between June and October.

How to get there
Madikwe is accessible by road and air. It lies 360 kilometres from Johannesburg (a comfortable four-hour drive). Federal Air runs daily flights from Oliver Tambo International in Johannesburg to the Madikwe airstrip.

Who to contact
Tel. (+27-31) 229 29 9555,
e-mail *info@morukuru.com*
or go to *www.morukuru.com*

royal madikwe
luxury safari residence

With accommodation fit for royalty and a malaria-free wildlife paradise on its doorstep, this lodge is popular with guests who require discreet service and complete privacy.

After much pointing and gesturing, we locate a group
of rhinos in the undergrowth

PREVIOUS SPREAD Dinners around the long dining table are
grand, but festive affairs.

Delicate grass heads sway in the bushveld breeze.

THIS SPREAD An informal dinner beneath the stars.

A close encounter with the majestic rhinos.

The lodge's beautiful free-form pool seems part of the bush.

No expense has been spared in the provision of comfort for the guests,
from the deep, comfortable beds to the inviting couches.

The staff at Royal Madikwe are friendly and the service is flawless. Here,
they prepare to serve dinner on a private deck.

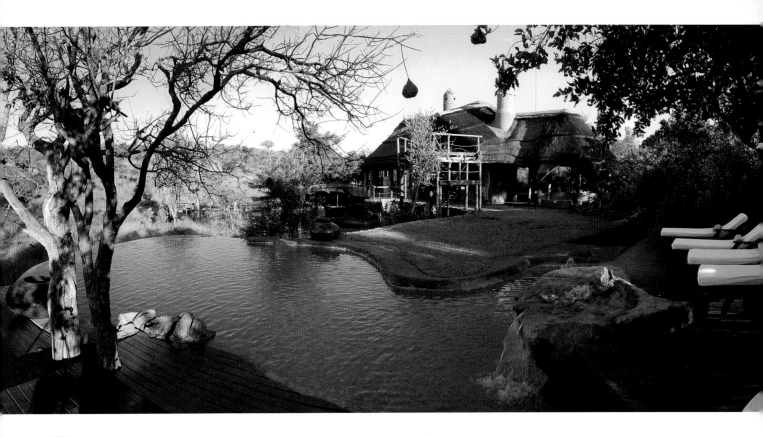

Our vehicle climbs the dolerite hill, then peaks and descends, rolling downwards along a pretty, winding road. Nearing the bottom, we hear voices singing. It's the team from Royal Madikwe welcoming us with an African serenade. I feel like royalty on a state visit.

Royal Madikwe is a luxury safari residence set on the edge of its own private valley with a natural waterhole at its centre. Greeting me, managers Riaan and Stephanie Kruger explain that the lodge comprises four luxury suites and one Royal Family suite, each with its own plunge pool to cool off in after exploring the bush. It's clearly and unashamedly opulent and, while being escorted to my own patch of paradise, I am told that the staff here are totally flexible, and will tailor activities to your every need. The reserve is also malaria free.

I've spent the past few dawn hours bumping about in a car, so I request a bush walk. Others will join me, I'm told, and a time is set. I anticipate with enthusiasm the exercise and the opportunity to experience the feel and smells of the bush.

Soon the 4x4 vehicle arrives and we're transported to a spot known to be good for walking. We clamber out and, after just a few minutes of strolling through the bushes, Dinamosi Malhenze, the eagle-eyed Shangaan tracker, catches sight of the ear of a rhino twitching just 200 metres away in the grass. Naturally, none of us is able to see anything but, after much pointing and gesturing, we locate a group of rhinos in the undergrowth. Riaan checks the wind direction and whispers an invitation to approach the juggernauts up close. Some of the group have never been close to a large wild animal before, and the adrenalin surging through us is almost tangible.

Riaan briefs us quickly, but thoroughly, on safety and etiquette, and we creep across the grassy ground. Within 50 metres of the rhinos, a cluster of oxpeckers flies off in alarm. Holding our breath, we stand our ground and marvel at the animals. Then we turn and head back to our vehicle. What an experience!

Back at the lodge, breakfast is being served on the outside deck and we settle down to a meal fit for a king, while watching a herd of zebras pass in front of the deck. Meals at Royal Madikwe can be taken in a number of venues, from the open-air boma to the deck above the waterhole. In the evening, these dining areas are transformed into a fairytale setting, with lights, immaculate linen and sparkling crystal. Dining beneath the sequinned African sky is an unforgettable experience.

On the upper deck, a large telescope has been set up. On clear nights, after a fine meal and with a glass of brandy or amarula liqueur in hand, it's wonderful to examine a close-up view of the firmament, tracking the stars and planets. After dinner, which includes the most succulent piece of fillet I've ever tasted, I plan my return visit.

details

When to go
Royal Madikwe is a year-round destination. Summers are hot, with afternoon thundershowers, and winters are cold and dry. Game-viewing is best between June and October.

How to get there
Madikwe lies 360 kilometres from Johannesburg (a comfortable four-hour drive). Federal Air runs daily flights from Oliver Tambo International Airport to the Madikwe airstrip. Private air charters can be arranged.

Who to contact
Tel. (+27-82) 787 1314/568 8867, e-mail *reservations@ royalmadikwe.com* or go to *www.royalmadikwe.com*

tuningi
safari lodge

It's impossible not to fall in love with Tuningi and

its irresistible combination of family-friendly facilities,

laid-back chic and spectacular wildlife.

Wide-armed, with warm smiles, lodge manager-ess Heidi and ranger Gavin greet me as I arrive at Tuningi. Chatting cheerfully, they escort me into the thatched main lodge, past a large fig tree *Ficus thonningii*, after which the lodge is named. Meals are often served beneath its canopy of branches, I am told. Inside, the lodge buzzes with the mingled chatter of an eclectic selection of guests – a British family, a high-spirited group of Italian advertisement producers and a young honeymoon couple. The mood is happy and the camaraderie is evident. I know I'm in for a great time.

Tuningi Safari Lodge lies at the top of a valley in the south-western edge of Madikwe Game Reserve. Just 16 guests are accommodated at a time. All the rooms are furnished elegantly and comfortably in a style known as 'colonial African chic'. Each has spectacular views.

Madikwe has a reputation for being one of the best places in South Africa to see the rare and endangered African wild dog. Shortly after settling in, I join some of the other guests on a game drive. While watching a pair of black-backed jackals, Grant, our guide, receives a message that a big pack of 17 wild dogs has been spotted. Knowing how fast the canines can move and the importance of this sighting, he tells us all to hang on tightly as he picks up the pace. Exhilarated, we cling to the 4x4's body-work, bouncing through the bush with the wind in our hair.

We reach the pack just after it has dispatched a young wildebeest and the dogs are tucking into their kill with gusto. Thinking we have missed the main part of the action, Grant positions the vehicle to afford us a good view of the dogs who have spread out, and are resting. Suddenly, the dogs start

Madikwe has a reputation for being one of the best places in South Africa to see the rare and endangered African wild dog

their characteristic chirping, then jump up and excitedly make a dash for a single wildebeest mother and her calf. We watch, mesmerised, as two wilde-beest unite to try to defend the youngster. They suc-ceed in driving off the attackers and escort the calf to safety. The children in the vehicle whoop with excitement, pleased with the happy ending!

Little Tuningi is a small camp that is separate from the main lodge. Here, the honeymoon couple was tucked away, assured of complete privacy. This camp accommodates just six people, and has its own private kitchen, boma area, swimming pool and exclusive waterhole. The Italian party was comfort-ably located on the western side of the camp where they had three double rooms, and the British family of five were in one of the two special family units.

Tuningi is one of the few top-quality child-friendly lodges in South Africa. Heidi is an expert at entertaining children, and has designed a pro-gramme to keep kids 'bush busy' for weeks. I found youngsters making animal-print T-shirts and identifying tracks and spoor. After dinner, I browse through the guest book. There I see one of the best compliments I've ever encountered of a retreat like this. It was written by a child, who said: 'I would give up my entire year's pocket money to come back here'. I know how he felt.

PREVIOUS SPREAD Subtle lighting in the lodge's lounge illuminates the flowing veranda and swimming pool.

THIS SPREAD The thatched rooms are thoughtfully furnished with deeply welcoming beds and comfortable seating.

A weaver building its nest. Birdwatching in the Madikwe reserve is particularly rewarding.

After a game drive on a hot summer morning, a dip in Tuningi's beautiful pool is essential.

A bath with a view.

African wild dogs.

details

When to go
Tuningi is a year-round destination. Summers are hot, with afternoon thundershowers, and winters are cold and dry. Game-viewing is best between June and October.

How to get there
Madikwe is accessible by road and air. It is 360 kilometres from Johannesburg (a four-hour drive). Federal Air runs daily flights from Oliver Tambo International Airport to the Madikwe airstrip.

Who to contact
For more information and reservations, tel. (+27-11) 805 9995, e-mail *reservations@madikwecollection.com* or go to *www.madikwecollection.com*

gauteng, limpopo & north west

Summer thunderstorms over Johannesburg.

JOHN HONE/AFRICAIMAGERY.COM

IF JOHANNESBURG is your first port of call, you've come to a shopper's paradise. There are also interesting museums here, and a visit to Zoo Lake and its tranquil gardens is a must. To the north, pretty Pretoria is known as Jacaranda City.

Just a short drive out of the city will bring you to Pilanesberg Game Reserve and its prolific wildlife, and glittering Sun City, a playground of golf, gambling and nonstop entertainment.

For a more remote bush escape, head north into the Waterberg, with its host of luxury lodges to choose from – all offering superb wildlife experiences in a scenic, mountainous terrain. Further west, on the border with Botswana, is Madikwe Game Reserve, with its Big Five and luxurious private lodges.

For itinerary suggestions, contact:
AFRICA GEOGRAPHIC TRAVEL
Tel. (+27-21) 762 2180
E-mail *travel@africageographic.com*
Website *www.africageographictravel.com*

Johannesburg

Zoo Lake Stroll around the gardens and enjoy the peace at Zoo Lake, a municipal garden in the city's northern suburbs. You can even take to the water in a hired paddle boat. During the first weekend of the month, there's an exhibition by local artists. There's also a restaurant for when hunger pangs strike.

Walter Sisulu National Botanical Garden Lovers of flora will enjoy the rare indigenous plants growing in this 300-hectare reserve. The gardens are also home to 220 bird species, a number of reptiles, and mammals, such as small antelope and jackals.

Gold Reef City Visit this theme park, with its exhilarating rides and slides. If that's not for you, take a ride into an old gold-mine shaft and learn about the history of mining. There's also lots to see at the Gold Reef City museums.

Apartheid Museum Get to know more about South Africa's political history at this fascinating museum.

Montecasino Montecasino complex is designed to represent a Tuscan village, with authentic buildings and cobbled walkways. This is the place to be seen – and there are trendy coffee shops, restaurants, stylish bars and sumptuous shopping.

Lion Park Drive around the 300-hectare Lion Park to see the lions interact, feed, play and sleep. The restaurant in the park is open seven days a week.

Pretoria

In central Pretoria, you'll find the beautiful National Zoological Gardens, home to the largest zoo in the country and the Aquarium and Reptile Park. Every October, the city is transformed into a wonderland when millions of lilac and purple blossoms fall from its 70 000 jacaranda trees to form pools on the roads and pavements – contact the tourist bureau for a map of the Jacaranda Route. There's plenty for museum buffs, too, with the Kruger House Museum, Melrose House, the Museum of Science and Technology, and the Pierneef Museum, dedicated to the life and work of South Africa's best-known landscape painter.

Sterkfontein Caves

Near Krugersdorp, a vast network of caves is world-famous for its fossil finds, including the fossilised skull of 'Mrs Ples', estimated to be more than two million years old. There are

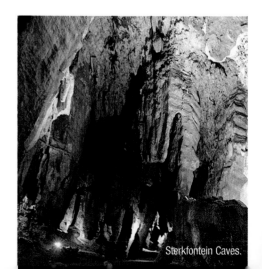

Sterkfontein Caves.

guided tours into the labyrinth, taking in the 23-metre-high Hall of Elephants and a crystal-clear underground lake. The caves are a World Heritage Site.

Hartbeesport Dam

This enormous sheet of water beneath the Magaliesberg mountains is one of the highveld's best recreation spots. At weekends, city dwellers flock here to enjoy a host of watersports, or to picnic on its shores. Drive around the dam to admire the views, then have a meal at one of the restaurants at the water's edge.

Madikwe Game Reserve

Madikwe comprises 75 000 hectares of bushland in North West Province, abutting the Kalahari Desert and the Botswana border. Regarded as one of the finest conservation areas in Africa, the reserve has all the major species, including the Big Five and most of the plains antelopes. Numerous private lodges in Madikwe offer high-quality accommodation and game viewing.

Sun City

Visit this fantasy playground with its four luxurious hotels, entertainment complex, gaming centre, golf courses, man-made lake and exciting Valley of the Waves, where realistic turquoise breakers crash onto a white, palm-fringed beach.

Sun City.

ROGER DE LA HARPE (2)

Pilanesberg Game Reserve

A thousand-million years ago, this area was an active volcano. Today, Pilanesberg, next to Sun City, is one of the largest wildlife parks in South Africa, and provides sanctuary to numerous game, including the Big Five.

Waterberg

The Waterberg mountain range, incorporating many rivers, streams and swamps, sweeps for 150 kilometres from Thabazimbi in the west to Potgietersrus in the east. The scenery here is spectacular, and there are many game sanctuaries, nature reserves and farms along its reach. The big game species to be seen include elephant, lion, white and black rhino, hippo, leopard and buffalo, and it is a birdwatchers' paradise with more than 300 bird species. The Waterberg is steeped in history and some artefacts found here date back to the Stone Age.

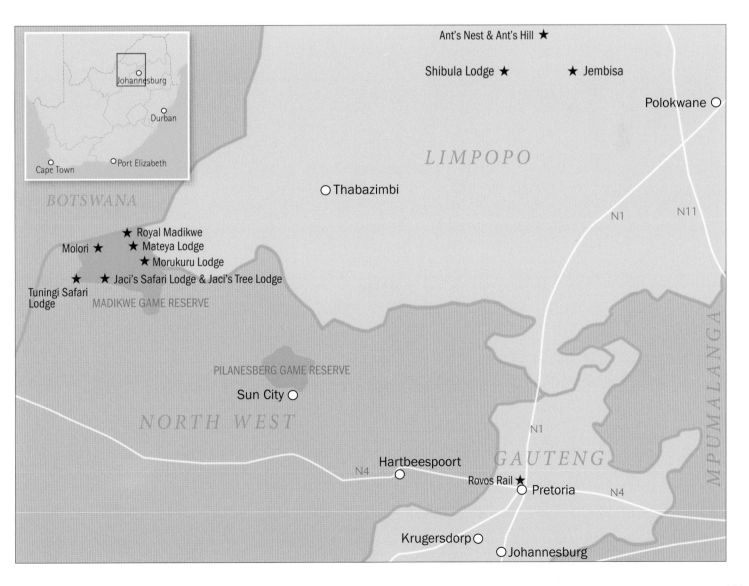

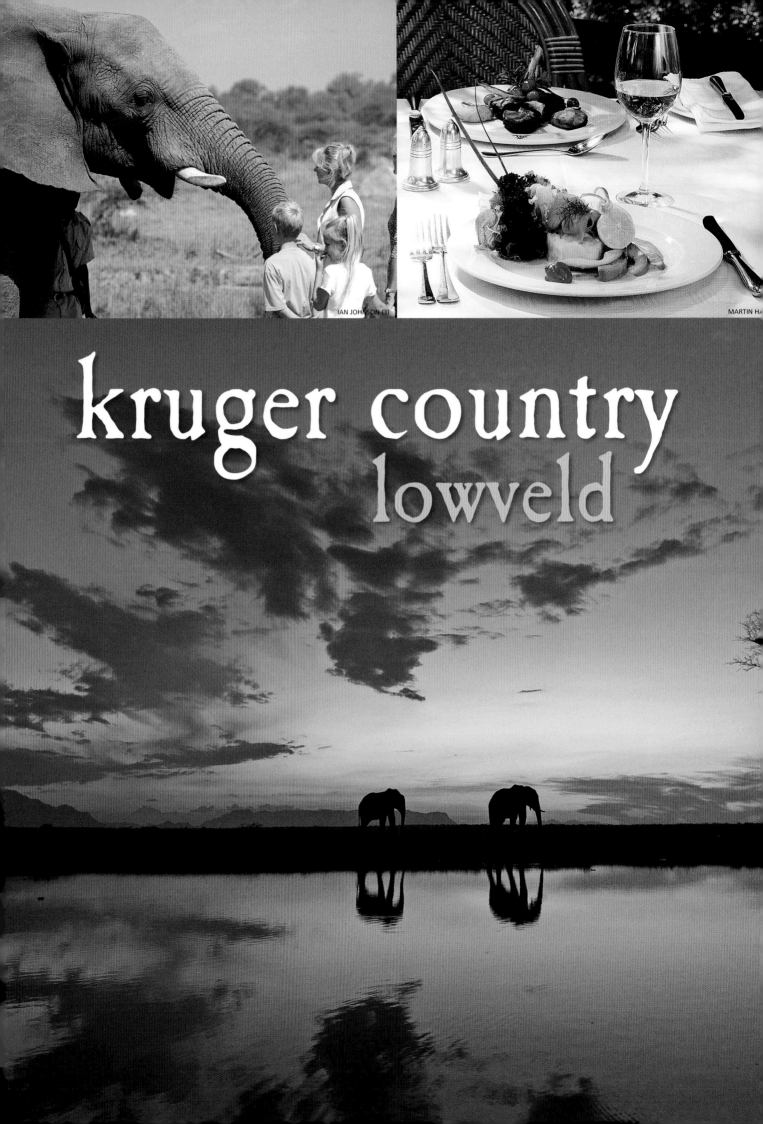

kruger country
lowveld

MARTIN HARVEY

Elephants at Camp Jabulani.

Big-game hunters once thundered on horseback across these hot and bushy plains, and prospectors, desperate to make their fortunes, flocked to the gold-mining camps that sprang up in the hills around Pilgrim's Rest and Sabie. Today the lowveld is best known as home to the Big Five and for the Kruger National Park, one of the great natural sanctuaries of the world. Beyond its western fence, a bouquet of excellent reserves offer diverse wildlife and five-star accommodation.

summerfields
river lodge & rose spa

Birdsong and the perfume of 35 000 roses fill the air at this seductive getaway on the Sabie River.

We pulled up at the entrance to Summerfields and opened our car doors to the welcoming fragrance of roses of every type and colour. Travel-weary, we inhaled the luscious scent as we were led to our suite. It was everything we needed: rustic in atmosphere, but caringly appointed with fine percale linen and generous bowls of beautiful roses.

The suites at Summerfields are built on wooden platforms that jut out over the Sabie River gorge, and our bay window revealed a spectacular view. Within minutes we had finished the macadamia nuts, tastefully presented in a pewter bowl, and were scanning the spa menu. We'd been tipped off that a trip to Summerfields would be incomplete without enjoying at least one self-indulgent session at the Rose Spa, which is built in Balinese open-plan style on the banks of the river. We looked forward to enjoying a massage while listening to the birdcalls, the cascading water and the snort and snuffle of a wallowing hippo.

Bathing in the privacy of our suite also held promise. While eating dinner, guests can order special-menu baths to be drawn in their own luxury bathrooms. Each bath is accompanied with complementary drinks and delicacies to match your choice of treatment. To ensure a good night's sleep, you could be served home-baked good-mood cookies and a specially infused tea to aid digestion and wellbeing, while soaking in a tub with a blend of calming oils. A rose-milk bath for two, with champagne and Belgian chocolates, is guaranteed to inspire romance.

We strolled to the restaurant for dinner, and sat in candlelit splendour with roses on the table and a view of the trees

Established by the owners André and IIse van Heerden to combine a working farm with a guest retreat, the lodge is situated on a 100-hectare farm beside Mpumalanga's Sabie River. Some 35 000 rose bushes, grown in greenhouses, provide long-stem blooms for sale in South Africa. The couple also grow macadamia nuts, which are used in the kitchen and spa, and are sold abroad.

From the lodge, wooden walkways stretch sinuously through lush bushveld heavily treed with jackalberry and tamboti. It was very pleasant to wander along, listening to the birds and observing the small creatures of the undergrowth. Other activities on offer include trips to nearby Kruger National Park (it's just 10 kilometres away), horse and quad-bike trails, hot-air ballooning, river rafting, microlight flights, geckoing (tubing on the river in a small raft that is steered using webbed gloves), waterfall abseiling, a visit to a tree-canopy aerial walkway, and, for those passionate gardeners who visit, a tour of the rose farm.

Another delightful surprise was the quality of the cuisine; we think that the chef here must be the region's best-kept secret. After a rest, we strolled to the restaurant for dinner, and sat in candlelit splendour with roses on the table and a view of the trees. We dined on asparagus bavarois with an orange hollandaise sauce, rocket salad with roasted cherry tomatoes and parmesan shavings, lamb cutlets with rosemary potatoes and, to finish, a delicious pavlova with Chantilly cream. The menu is prepared by chef Lienkie Erasmus, who has worked extensively both locally and abroad. She takes her inspiration from the freshest produce in season, which is supplied by local farmers and the restaurant's own garden. Everything from chutneys, mayonnaise and bread is homemade. 'I keep everything simple and fresh,' she told us.

PREVIOUS SPREAD High-quality cuisine is prepared under the watchful eye of chef Lienkie Erasmus.

A rose-petal-filled bath is the essence of romance.

THIS SPREAD The spa overlooks the bushveld and the Sabie River.

The air is filled with the heady scent of Summerfields' profusion of roses.

Waiting for a massage.

You could lose yourself in the view from your poolside lounger.

The tented suites offer all the creature comforts.

details

When to go
Open all year. However, temperatures can soar between November and February.

How to get there
About 450 kilometres from Johannesburg, Summerfields lies about five kilometres from Hazyview on the R536 towards Sabie. Daily scheduled flights from Johannesburg, Durban and Cape Town fly into Kruger Mpumalanga International Airport. Transfers to the lodge can be arranged.

Who to contact
Tel. (+27-13) 737 6500, e-mail *reservations@summerfields.co.za* or go to *www.summerfields.co.za*

lion sands
private game reserve

This private concession in the Sabi Sand Game Reserve
spans 10 kilometres of game-rich Sabie River frontage.
Its two accommodation options, River Lodge and Ivory
Lodge, offer guests their own patch of wildlife paradise.

Once a ranger has
dropped you off, it's
just you, the moon,
your picnic dinner and
the animals

PREVIOUS SPREAD Lamplit dinners in the boma are popular with
guests at Lion Sands.

THIS SPREAD Ivory Lodge's villas have private wooden verandas
and a heated swimming pool.

You can see the wildlife without leaving your Ivory Lodge bed.

A white rhino. Males usually weigh more than 2 000 kilograms.

The lodge is known for its five-star cuisine.

The central lounge, where guests meet and new
friends are made.

As we entered the deeply thatched reception area, a beaming waiter greeted us with large, bedewed glasses of iced tea. 'Welcome,' he said, beckoning us inside. I'd heard that River Lodge prides itself on making guests feel at home, and I felt the troubles of the world melt away as I surrendered myself into its capable hands.

The lodge is the first to have been constructed in Lion Sands, in the southern section of the Sabi Sand Game Reserve. It is situated among trees, some of which are 800 years old, on the banks of the meandering Sabie River.

We were led along a slatted wooden promenade to our accommodation, one of 18 thatched, air-conditioned rooms, with a king-sized bed, generous mosquito nets, comfortable armchairs with squashy cushions, and a sumptuous bathroom with an attractive pebble floor. Outside, our private viewing deck overlooked the river. On the bed, flowers and a personalised note welcomed us to the lodge.

After a rest, we took a late-afternoon game drive. Big Five sightings are almost assured at Lion Sands and our ranger told us about a rare spectacle that had been witnessed by recent visitors. An elephant had given birth right in front of the game-drive vehicle. 'An elephant's gestation period is 22 months,' he told us, 'so for us to be in the exact spot that she was giving birth was a real stroke of luck.' We weren't as fortunate, but we saw other elephants and buffaloes, as well as giraffes and a rainbow collection of birds.

Later, in the central lounge area, we swopped sightings with other guests, whom, we discovered, were to spend that evening in the Chalkley Treehouse, a platform built in a 500-year-old leadwood tree some distance from the main lodge. Here they would sleep, high above the ground, in four-poster comfort, with fine linen – and nothing but a mosquito net to separate them from the stars. Once a ranger has dropped you off, they told me, it's just you, the moon, your picnic dinner and the animals wandering beneath the platform. I felt quite envious.

River Lodge's twin getaway, the award-winning Ivory Lodge, offers one of the most sumptuous wildlife experiences that money can buy. I stood at the entrance to my private villa, one of just six at Ivory Lodge, and gazed around the room, taking in the dark-wood bed, pristine white linen, beautifully draped mosquito netting and carved couches. I wandered into the bathroom, where a deep, oval sandstone tub stood, surrounded by glass walls and a forest of candles, and beyond to an oversized outside shower. Ivory Lodge is, indeed, luxury at its finest.

Each thatched villa has a front wall of glass that overlooks the Sabie River and every nuance of the Lion Sands bushveld. Even the bed is perfectly positioned to allow you to watch the passing parade without emerging from the covers. Outside, there's a private wooden deck and heated infinity pool.

I strolled along to the central area, where I explored the library for a book about the local animals, and scanned a list of the activities offered. Guests can investigate the lowveld night sky, take nature walks by night or day, explore the plentiful wildlife on a game drive, take the hippopotamus tour, enjoy a picnic lunch in the bush or attend a wildlife lecture. I wished I could stay for longer.

At the curio shop, a trove of items was displayed to serve as memories of the trip. My mementos will be the chance viewings I had from my villa: the baby elephant bathing; the crocodile that slid by, its eyes perusing the riverbank for an unsuspecting victim; the herd of zebras that lapped water delicately, always alert to danger.

details

When to go
River Lodge and Ivory Lodge are open all year. The summer months (November to February) can be very hot.

How to get there
Lion Sands Private Game Reserve is some 520 kilometres by road from Johannesburg. For guests arriving by air, Airlink offers direct flights from Johannesburg, Durban and Cape Town to Sabi Sand reserve. Road transfers to the lodges can be arranged.

Who to contact
Tel. (+27-11) 484 9911, fax (+27-11) 484 9916, e-mail *res@lionsands.com* or go to *www.lionsands.com*

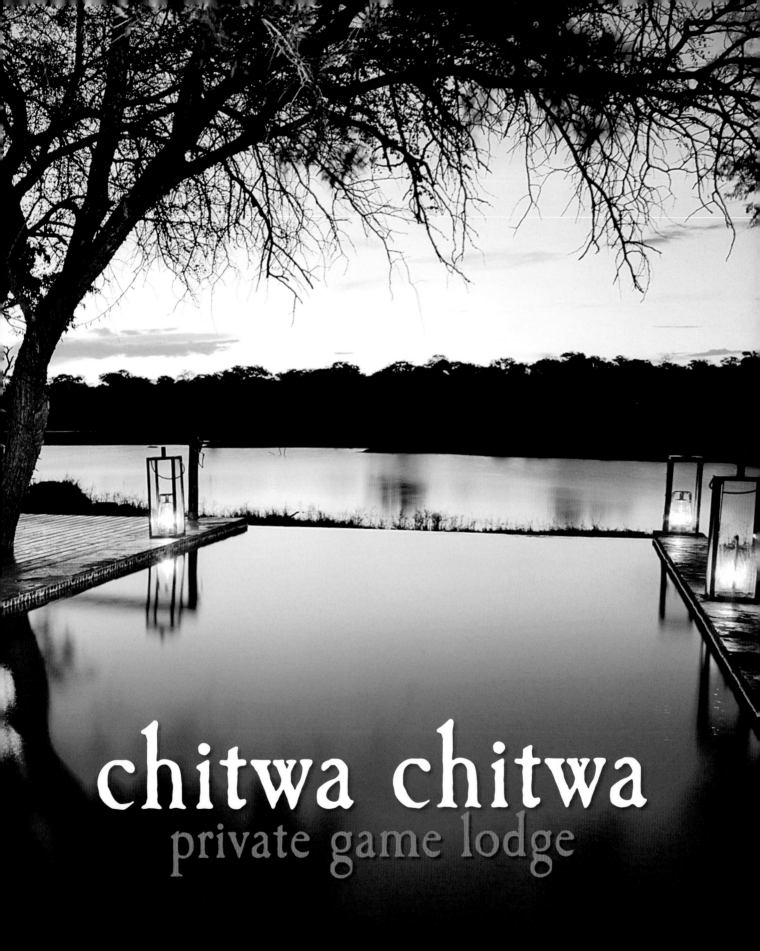

chitwa chitwa
private game lodge

This spacious lodge bordering the Kruger National Park engenders fond memories of hot

lowveld days, magnificent wildlife, great food and beds you could sleep in forever.

Animals come here to drink in the morning and evening
... and the water is home to hippos and crocodiles

PREVIOUS SPREAD Lamps reflected in the pool and river create
an evening wonderland.

THIS SPREAD Chitwa Chitwa overlooks the largest dam in the Sabi Sand
Game Reserve, which attracts wild animals day and night.

The bar and lounge area – the perfect place to unwind after a day
in the bush.

Two rhinos. Game drives at Chitwa Chitwa are always rewarding.

Fine food and the best wines are the order of the day in the dining room.

Crisp linens, elegant furniture and outsized
beds guarantee a restful stay.

Browsing through the guest book, my attention was caught by an entry that described the visitor's memories as 'affectionate'. I wondered if Chitwa Chitwa would have the same effect on me.

On arrival at the lodge, which is situated in the beautiful Sabi Sand Game Reserve, we were greeted with fresh fruit juice by the smiling managers and staff. We would be staying at Game Lodge, they told us. The exuberant owners of this lovely lodge also made us feel at home from the moment we stepped through the door. And, as we witnessed later, the couple greeted all arrivals as though they were longed-for visitors rather than paying guests.

We were led to our thatched chalet, one of eight, and I stood for a while admiring the surroundings. Designed with finesse, the furniture was elegant, with touches of Africa in the fabrics and artefacts. The huge, king-sized bed was dressed in crisp cotton and swathed with romantic (and effective) mosquito netting. Behind floor to ceiling glass, a deep Jacuzzi beckoned.

Outside, a private terrace and plunge pool overlooked the surrounding bushveld and the largest dam in the Sabi Sand, providing an intriguing vantage point for game-viewing. Animals come here to drink in the morning and evening, I was told, and the water is home to hippos and crocodiles. Sighing at the pleasures that awaited us, we unpacked our bags and headed back to the main lodge.

The bar and lounge area melt into the surrounding trees, and we were invited to take a seat in the thatched, open-air boma for lunch. Cuisine at Chitwa Chitwa focuses on African and Mediterranean dishes and, suddenly hungry, we tucked in with gusto.

Later, after an afternoon nap that was disturbed only by birdcalls and the sounds of the hot lowveld bush, we joined a group for a game drive. The ranger was determined that we see as much wildlife as possible, and within a short period we encountered elephants and wildebeest. This is Big Five country. All five didn't all appear, but we were entranced by the clever African wild dogs, elegantly striped zebras and wily baboons. There were antelope in vast quantities and a myriad birds. Sabi Sand has an unfenced boundary with the Kruger National Park, allowing the animals free passage. There is a lot to see, and our ranger had an encyclopedic knowledge of the surroundings.

We returned to the lodge for dinner. A brief visit to the chalet revealed that the bed had been prepared. However, hunger pangs proved the greater lure, and we hurried back to the boma, where an old tree stump in the middle of the tables bore a host of dazzling candles, and the waxy remains of their predecessors, which had illumined hundreds of sumptuous meals enjoyed beneath the stars. The conversation sparkled too, as the guests compared their sightings of the day. Dinner can also be served in the dining room, with its eye-catching artwork.

Back at our chalet, we took a dip in the lantern-lit plunge pool and raised a toast to the African night. My memories of Chitwa Chitwa Game Lodge would also be fond.

details

When to go
Chitwa Chitwa is open all year. Temperatures can be extremely high between November and February.

How to get there
Fly-in packages are arranged by the lodge, which has its own airstrip. By road, Chitwa Chitwa lies some 600 kilometres (about six hours) from Johannesburg, an easy drive on national roads.

Who to contact
Tel. (+27-13) 744 0876/3749 (head office) or (+27-13) 735 5357 (lodge). E-mail *reservations@chitwa.co.za* or go to *www.chitwa.co.za*

sabi sabi
earth lodge & bush lodge

This pristine oasis is tucked into a corner of the Sabi Sand Game Reserve.

Of the various accommodation options available, Bush Lodge is warm and

welcoming, while elegant Earth Lodge is the reserve's flagship retreat.

Earth Lodge

As we unpacked our belongings, marvelling at the luxuriousness of our accommodation, a movement outside the window caught my eye. There, strolling in front of our veranda, was a large elephant. Without glancing left or right, it passed out of sight, leaving us open-mouthed.

Earth Lodge is one of four luxurious retreats in the Sabi Sabi Private Game Reserve (the others are Bush Lodge, Selati Camp and Little Bush Camp). Described as the most environmentally sensitive lodge in Africa, it has been sculpted into the earth so subtly as to be almost invisible to the naked eye.

Our suite was one of 13, with gleaming patios, a plunge pool and rustic outside shower. Inside, however, little could be described as rustic. Crisp linen covered the king-sized bed, its headboard carved from a petrified tree. Persian rugs, the well-stocked bar and easy chairs made it almost unbearable to leave. However, we managed to emerge to take a dip in the pool, overlooking the bush. Our only interruption was the arrival of another large pachyderm. She grazed quietly as we watched, a captive audience until she lumbered away. And we had yet to step into a Land Rover!

Later, relaxed, we took a game drive, and were rewarded with sightings of cats and majestic buffaloes, which, we think, are the cream of the Big Five. We returned for dinner, which was served at a table for two at the waterhole. There, we dined on heavenly game, rounding off with a flourish – the chef's unique cheesecake.

Bush Lodge

Bush Lodge conveys a sense of warmth from the minute you step through the door. We loved its high, thatched ceilings, polished floors, plush oriental carpets and leather furnishings – a carefully designed meeting of safari and stylish hospitality.

At the front of the main lodge, a wooden deck overlooks the watering hole. Sabi Sabi is home to more than the Big Five – there are also cheetahs, African wild dogs and some 200 other animal species. The reserve is unfenced, so the animals roam freely. 'There is nothing quite as stirring as the sight of a lion, elephant or rhino roaming free in the bush, or as haunting as the sound of a hyaena laughing in the dead of the night,' we were told.

In our suite, one of 25, dramatic mosquito nets shrouded the bed, the slate floor was cool underfoot, and the bathroom sported a sunken bath. Outside, monkeys chattered in the trees.

A blast on a kudu horn summoned us to dinner. Later, guests returning from a safari told us about their exciting sightings – leopards, cheetahs, lions, baboons and white rhino. The experience was topped, they said, by a dinner prepared for them under the stars. We listened with a touch of envy, then wandered back to a dreamless sleep in our suite. Outside, the velvety night's silence was broken only by the crunch of elephant footsteps.

PREVIOUS SPREAD Award-winning Earth Lodge's organic architecture merges sensitively with its surroundings.

THIS SPREAD Normally slow-moving, the elephant can run at a speed of up to 40 kilometres per hour.

Enjoy a rock massage in the Zen garden.

The suites at Earth Lodge are almost too good to leave.

Dinner for two at a waterhole.

The entrance to Bush Lodge, admired for its warmth and home-from-home appeal.

SABI SABI

'There is nothing quite ...
as haunting as the sound
of a hyaena laughing in
the dead of the night'

details

When to go
Earth Lodge and Bush Lodge are open all year. Summers are hot; in winter, days are mild and nights are cold.

How to get there
There are daily scheduled flights from Oliver Tambo International Airport in Johannesburg to Kruger Mpumalanga International Airport, from where it's a short hop to the Sabi Sabi airstrip. Federal Air offers three chartered flights to the airstrip every day. The lodges are about five hours by road from Johannesburg.

Who to contact
Sabi Sabi head office,
tel. (+27-11) 447 7172,
e-mail *res@sabisabi.com*
or go to *www.sabisabi.com*

savanna
private game reserve

A menagerie of birds, the must-see Big Five

and other beasts await visitors to this small,

exclusive sanctuary in the Sabi Sand Reserve.

A late-afternoon game drive revealed not only big cats, but also a herd of lazy buffaloes and a trio of alert rhinos

In a 2007 report commissioned by the the Cape Leopard Trust, two members of the South African Leopard Forum stated: 'The Sabi Sand Reserve is one of the best places on earth to observe leopards in their natural habitat.' And they weren't wrong. Here, at Savanna Private Game Reserve, within the boundaries of the Sabi Sand and bordering the Kruger National Park, the game rangers seem to conjure the five 'must-see' animals out of thin air. From the safety of our Land Rover, we watched for 30 minutes as a male lion dozed and lazed in the afternoon sun, offering us unbeatable close-up views. We moved off to escape the heat and, within moments, came across a female leopard, draped languidly in the branches of a tree, also sheltering from the sun. Watching her, we wondered if the proximity of her ancient adversary, the lion, kept her in her arboreal resting place.

Savanna is not a super-luxurious boutique hotel. Instead, this small and exclusive lodge offers a refreshing escape from the hurly-burly of city life. Manager Paddy Hagelthorn and his team love their jobs, and will leave no stone unturned to ensure that you have a wildlife and bush experience second to none.

The suites, half permanent and half of tented construction, are welcoming and comfortable. Ours had a massive bed and two matching loungers with bolsters and scatter cushions, angled to ensure the best view of our very own corner of veld just beyond the door. Our private splash pool, ringed with hurricane lamps, enhanced an already romantic setting, and we looked forward to settling down to a meal at a table laid for two. We started the evening with two glasses of sherry and, after dinner, wallowed in the bubble-filled bath prepared by the staff.

The common area beckoned at the end of a long game drive. We admired the loft library, with its groaning bookshelves, inviting chairs and extraordinary views. In the lounge, a thatched, open-fronted room with cosy seating, guests can sip their drinks and compare their day's sightings while keeping an eye on the waterhole in front of the lodge.

On our final day, a late-afternoon game drive revealed not only big cats but also a herd of lazy buffaloes lounging in the veld and a trio of alert rhinos, causing the occupants of our Land Rover to fall into stunned silence (there are also elephant, hippo and crocodile, plus over 360 bird species to please ardent wildlife lovers).

Later, we returned beneath a typically spectacular African sunset of lilacs and golds to a real feast. The food was wholesome and delicious, and we fell on it. Loaves of home-made bread, freshly baked every day, disappeared as they did at each mealtime, and at the candlelit boma dinners. We sat at the fireside late into the night, listening to Paddy as he regaled us with action-filled stories.

PREVIOUS SPREAD A warm fire and plump armchairs encourage visitors to sit for a while.

A lucky sighting. A leopard shelters in a tree.

THIS SPREAD A brown-hooded kingfisher. This bird inhabits forest margins.

At night, lanterns transform the suites into a fairyland.

When it gets too hot, this lion will move to shelter in long grass or beneath a tree.

A bathroom fit for a movie star.

Dinnertime at the boma.

details

When to go
Savanna is open all year. However, temperatures can become uncomfortably hot between November and February.

How to get there
Daily scheduled flights from Johannesburg, Durban and Cape Town fly into Kruger Mpumalanga International Airport. Alternatively, you can fly from Johannesburg directly to the Sabi Sand Game Reserve. Transfers can be arranged. By road, the lodge is about 480 kilometres from Johannesburg.

Who to contact
Tel. (+27-13) 751 2474, fax (+27-13) 751 3620, e-mail *res@savannalodge.com* or go to *www.savannalodge.com*

tinga
private game lodge

Evening meals are often serenaded by local wildlife

at this tranquil retreat on the Sabie River.

Following my host, I head along the elevated wooden walkway that winds through the bush to my suite. He opens the door and I step across the hearth. Inside, I see gloriously extravagant drapes surrounding the super-sized bed, a comfortable seating area and a plush en-suite bathroom. I turn around and look out across the wooden deck and heated plunge pool to the gently flowing Sabie River. 'There are nine suites here at Narina Lodge,' he says. 'All of them overlook the river. That's where you'll see hippos and crocodiles.' I hope his prophecy comes true.

Tinga Private Game Lodge is situated in a 5 000-hectare private concession tucked away in the Kruger National Park at the meeting of the Sabie and Sand rivers. The Sabie River is at the heart of the lodge, and views of it can be had from every corner, even from the huge windows of the bathrooms. I imagine lying back in the elegant stone tub and seeing an elephant or a hippo behind the glass.

Narina is one of two lodges here. The other, Legends, also houses the main guest areas. It exudes the romantic atmosphere of a classic safari destination, from its cathedral-like thatched entrance to its colonial-style lounge and well-stocked library with plump leather armchairs and big fireplace. Outside, a huge wooden deck has been built around a 200-year-old jackalberry tree. It's here that guests congregate in the evenings, drinks in hand, to discuss their day's sightings and keep an eye on the river and its resident wildlife. Meals are often served on the deck.

There are also beauty therapists here, who offer luxurious facials and body treatments, and massages in the chalets or on the private decks (weather permitting).

One male decides we are a nuisance and trumpets and flaps his ears, and we retreat, with adrenalin rushing through our veins

After a swim, we join an early-evening game drive. We're accompanied by a tracker and guide, who scour the vegetation for stirrings and tracks. The Big Five occur here, and Tinga's vehicles are allowed to traverse the entire Kruger network of roads. The guides are extremely knowledgeable and point out everything from snake tracks to a small scorpion on a tree. We also see zebras, warthogs, swaying giraffes and elephants, and are privileged to follow a male leopard for several hundred metres. On our return, we catch sight of a herd of elephants crossing the river. Majestic matriarchs chivvy the youngsters along, shepherding them to the other side. One male decides we are a nuisance and trumpets and flaps his ears, and we retreat, with adrenalin rushing through our veins. Finally, we are treated to the the sight of a lioness suckling her cub. It's been one of the best game drives I've ever taken.

We return to dine on crocodile carpaccio, followed by kudu steaks with pesto. We end with a cheese platter of seemingly unending variety. The staff is discreet and professional, the wines are sublime. (In the unlikely event that the steward's choice of wine is not for you, guests are encouraged to peruse the private cellar for that special bottle.) It's the perfect end to a perfect day.

PREVIOUS SPREAD There's romance in every detail of Tinga's suites.

The food is excellent; the wines are from a well-stocked cellar.

THIS SPREAD Head to tail, a herd of elephants crosses the Sabie River.

The sitting room at Legends Lodge has an air of colonial elegance.

A massage on your private deck. Pampering facials and body treatments are popular after a long morning in pursuit of wildlife.

From the canopied bed, you can watch the ever-changing patterns of light on the bushveld.

A myriad lanterns illuminate an open-air barbecue.

details

When to go
Tinga is open all year. Temperatures can become extremely high between November and February.

How to get there
Airlink offers flights from Johannesburg, Cape Town and Durban to Kruger Mpumalanga International Airport near Nelspruit. By road, Tinga lies some 600 kilometres (about six hours) from Johannesburg, an easy drive on national roads.

Who to contact
Tel. (+27-13) 735 8400,
e-mail *reservations@tinga.co.za*
or go to *www.tinga.co.za*

ulusaba
private game reserve

Like a treehouse kingdom with a millionaire's touch,

Ulusaba straddles a hill overlooking 13 500 hectares

of pristine lowveld wilderness.

Sitting on the highest point in the Sabi Sand Game Reserve, I can see the surrounding landscape spread out beneath me. Two decades previously, when I started my career in the world of wildlife, I used to come to this spot to watch the more secretive animals: to listen for the roar that signalled the arrival of the king of all creatures, or look out for the shy herd of breeding elephants. The Shangaan people call this 560-metre hill *Ulusaba*, or 'Place of little fear', and used it as a vantage point from which to spy on their enemies. The private game reserve that now exists here bears its name.

Today, however, I've come to beautiful Ulusaba as a guest, and to stay in one of the luxury suites that dot the slopes of the rocky inselberg. My suite is named Makwela Dawn, after a well-known leopard that lives in the area. Ulusaba's Rock Lodge (its other is Safari Lodge) lies at the heart of her territory, and she raised her cubs in the shelter of these boulders.

Leopards were once rare in this part of the Sabi Sand, especially females, so I was keen to catch sight of one of these sleuth-like beasts. I expressed my interest, and before dawn the following morning, two guides collected me and we set off in a 4x4 vehicle into the bush. 'There's been a kill in a tree,' said Thulani Godi. Moving in the darkness, he spotted fresh lion tracks. Suddenly, there was a flurry and an

... I headed for the Aroma Boma, a thatched spa perched on tree-lined slopes above the lovely valley

explosion in the bush beside our vehicle, and a lioness leapt, growling, into a large marula tree. Three other lions followed, hot on her tail.

Looking up, we identified the cause of the lions' concern. There, in the tree's uppermost branches, sat Makwela, the female leopard, staring calmly at the commotion beneath her. The lioness, realising she was in the wrong place, dropped to the ground with an awkward twist and trotted off with her friends. Once they'd left, Makwela descended gracefully. She followed the entrance road to the lodge, taking the steep slope with ease, and headed into the rocks directly below my room. The last time I saw her, she was perched on a boulder, surveying her surroundings like a queen.

Ulusaba is a private game reserve second to none, and the guestbook is filled with quotes of praise and delight. My treehouse-style suite was the epitome of comfort, with glowing wooden floors, a deep, netting-swathed bed, a private pool on the veranda, and a sumptuous bathroom filled with an enticing range of toiletries.

The excitement of the morning had left me feeling tired, so I headed for the Aroma Boma, a thatched spa perched on tree-lined slopes above the lovely valley. An hour later, I returned to my room, meltingly relaxed. I strolled to the dining room and, beneath a many-tiered chandelier, was served tender beef fillet, with assorted fresh vegetables and the best South African wines. This lodge is owned by the UK entrepreneur Sir Richard Branson, and, in his distinctive style, he has ensured that every aspect of comfort and satisfaction has been covered. I raised a glass to toast my famous host, and to the beautiful leopard, and headed for the comfort of that deep, deep bed.

PREVIOUS SPREAD A lone elephant struts along a path beneath Rock Lodge.

The stilted deck and a tranquil pool ride high above the plains.

THIS SPREAD All the suites are built like treehouses, although rather more sophisticated than those of your childhood.

The bar seems to float above its surroundings.

Fresh-air massages are given on the balcony of the thatched Aroma Boma.

Makwela, the female leopard who reigns supreme at Ulusaba.

The beautiful dining area.

details

When to go
Ulusaba is open all year. Summer temperatures are high, while winter (May to September) brings moderately warm days and cool, crisp nights.

How to get there
Ulusaba is just a 80 minutes by air from Johannesburg. Daily scheduled and charter flights are available to the lodge's private airstrip.

Who to contact
Tel. (+27-11) 325 4405, e-mail *enquiries@ulusaba.virgin.com*
or go to *www.virgin.com/ulusaba*

camp
jabulani

It's little wonder that Camp Jabulani is popular with the wealthy.

It's five-star living includes spacious suites, cordon bleu cuisine

and lofty elephant-back rides through the lowveld bush.

We crossed a dry riverbed, rocking through territory no 4x4 could ever have managed. Beside me rode Kasweed Friday, a young Zimbabwean mahout, on his three-tonne friend Joe, an elephant – also from Zimbabwe. We ambled along, accompanied by the gentle pad of huge elephant feet on the ground, the crackle of the bush and the gentle tones of the mahout as he encouraged the great creatures along the path. We passed a well-hidden group of kudu, swaying giraffes and herds of zebra and wildebeest, all of whom acknowledged our presence with a mere glance before turning their attention back to the grazing.

At the head of our little entourage was a young elephant named Jabulani (which means 'happiness' in the Zulu language). Kasweed explained that, in 1997, Jabulani had become stuck in the mud of a silt dam and was abandoned by his herd. Lente Roode, the owner of Camp Jabulani, rescued the elephant and, over the course of a year, nursed him back to health. Five years later, 12 elephants in Zimbabwe were brought to South Africa when it was discovered that they had been tagged for bushmeat. Jabulani was immediately adopted by the newcomers.

Camp Jabulani was established to generate funds for the care of the elephants. And what a camp it is! All the superlatives apply here. It offers five-star luxury, excellent service, complete privacy and magnificent cuisine. It is popular with those who desire to escape from the prying eyes of the public, confident in the knowledge that their presence will be handled with discretion. Yet, despite its elegant grandeur, there's a wonderful 'home-from-home' atmosphere. My suite, one of just six, was unlike any other I'd ever seen, with a huge bed with fine cotton bedlinen, a massive bathtub that begged for oceans of bubbles and a glass of champagne, and indoor and outdoor showers. In winter, a fire is lit in the big fireplace, flanked by deep chairs in which to curl up with a good book.

During the day, the walls of the suite are rolled back to reveal an uninterrupted view of the bush and the game. And that isn't all. 'You have your own butler,' I was told. 'All you need to do is call him.' I could hardly bring myself to leave my room. I managed, however, and set off to the dining room for dinner.

The chef here is Rudolf van den Berg, for whom 'cooking is like music, a symphony of flavours'. My starter was sublime samosas with rolled, melt-in-the-mouth salmon, followed by tender venison fillets and, for dessert, a rosy baked pear with the smoothest vanilla ice cream I have ever tasted.

The following morning, I elected to visit the Hoedspruit Endangered Species Centre. Also created by the Roode family, the centre focuses on breeding programmes for rare and endangered species, including African wild dogs and cheetahs. Our guide introduced us to the pack habits of the wild dog and the inner workings of a vulture restaurant. He also showed us some new additions to the centre – a pair of blue crane chicks and, to our amusement, a young rhino who wallowed with enthusiasm in his bath.

On leaving, I cast my mind back to my stay at Camp Jabulani. It was perfect in every aspect. However, the single memory that leapt out above all others was my night-time elephant ride. The outing started with cocktails at Elephant Dam, and then, as the sun set, we climbed onto our mild-mannered mounts and strode into the dusk. Those night sounds of the African bush, intensified by the enveloping darkness, will stay with me forever.

PREVIOUS SPREAD Before embarking on an evening elephant-back ride, guests are served sundowners beside a tranquil dam.

THIS SPREAD Elephants have large feet that spread like cushions when they touch the ground, enabling the animals to move surprisingly silently through the bush.

Luxury at its best in the suites.

White-backed vulture.

Dinner awaits on the shaggy-thatched deck.

At night, a fire is lit in the cosy lounge to ward off the lowveld chill.

We ambled along, accompanied by the gentle pad of huge elephant feet on the ground

details

When to go
Camp Jabulani is open all year.

How to get there
South African Express runs daily scheduled flights between Eastgate Airport at Hoedspruit and both Oliver Tambo and Cape Town international airports. Private charter flights can also be arranged.

Who to contact
Tel. (+27-15) 793 1265, (+27-12) 460 5605 or (+27-82) 922 0120, e-mail *campjabulani@campjabulani.com* or *reservations@campjabulani.com*, or go to *www.campjabulani.com*

royal
malewane
safari lodge

From mahogany four-posters and deep pillows to

ambrosial dining and a multitude of game, this prime

lodge is the getaway destination you'll never forget.

We were joined at the water's edge by two elephants craving a drink. We sat completely still as they drank their fill

When looking back on a visit to a safari lodge, it's not usually the mealtimes that pop into one's mind first. However, sometimes they are so memorable that merely recalling them sets the salivary glands into action. That's certainly true of Royal Malewane, where the chef, John Jackson, presented one delicious meal after the other. Sweetcorn and chilli soup, smoked salmon and avocado with a perfect chilli mayonnaise, prawns wrapped in delicate pastry with Thai red curry sauce, melt-in-the-mouth impala fillet with fresh asparagus, braised leg of lamb with sweet potato croquettes, and spicy oxtail with creamy mashed potatoes.

The desserts were equally imaginative. My favourite was the mango ginger tart, which arrived perfectly accompanied by smooth papino ice cream. It's no wonder that Royal Malewane has earned many accolades, including the UK *Tatler* magazine's Best Safari Lodge award in 2006.

Royal Malewane Lodge is situated in its own private, 13 000-hectare reserve within Thornybush Game Reserve on the western fringe of the Kruger National Park. From the moment you step through the door, between the bronze cheetahs that stand guard there, the opening words from Isak Dinesen's novel *Out of Africa*, 'I had a farm in Africa', come to mind. The style is old-world colonial, with an emphasis on comfort. The main camp complex is the heart of the lodge, and its thatched-roof buildings house the library, dining and reception areas and the shop. There are rich antiques and Persian carpets throughout.

Elevated walkways link the main camp to six luxury suites, plus the elegant Royal and the Malewane suites (20 people can be accommodated in total). Each is free-standing and melts into the surrounding bush. All the units have a plunge pool on their balconies and views to eternity. Inside, there are mahogany four-poster beds with floaty mosquito netting, fluffy pillows and monogrammed bedlinen of a refined thread count. The bedroom/sitting room has a fireplace, which was lit for us every evening, and a soft, red Persian carpet that invited us to kick off our shoes. A stone-built bathroom with a Victorian bath was fronted by a glass wall that promised 24-hour wildlife viewing.

Apart from eating, the other pastime at Royal Malewane is, of course, the animals. We took an early-morning game drive with Wilson Masiya, a master tracker, and Juan Pinto, a highly qualified field guide. Wilson sat on the bonnet of the Land Rover and brought to our attention everything from elephants, buffaloes, lions and giraffes – easily spotted – down to a chameleon on a leafy branch and a mongoose scurrying into its hole.

A later, evening game drive turned up just as many treasures. After sundowners and snacks conjured from a bottomless basket, we headed back to the lodge, ready for another fine dinner. On the way, darkness fell, and we were shown how to use the stars for navigation.

However, our final game-viewing experience was not from a vehicle but while relaxing in our plunge pool. There, we were joined at the water's edge by two elephants craving a drink. We sat completely still as they drank their fill.

Later, we drowsily rested our heads on our pillows and fell asleep to the roar of lions in the velvety African night.

PREVIOUS SPREAD Royal Malewane's spa overlooks the wild outdoors, and is the perfect refuge for rejuvenation.

A shady corner of paradise.

THIS SPREAD A nyala female.

Two elephants treated our plunge pool as their personal water fountain.

One beautiful dish after the other emerged from the kitchen.

A thatched suite. At Royal Malewane, comfort is rated as highly as luxury.

Dinners can be held Bedouin-style in the bush.

details

When to go
Royal Malewane is a year-round destination. Summers are hot, with afternoon thundershowers, and winters are cold and dry. Game-viewing is best between June and October.

How to get there
There are daily flights from Johannesburg and Cape Town to Hoedspruit, Nelspruit and the Royal Malewane airstrip. Transfers can be arranged. The lodge lies some 600 kilometres (a six-hour drive) from Johannesburg.

Who to contact
Tel. (+27-15)793 0150, e-mail *info@royalmalewane.com* or go to *www.royalmalewane.com*

singita
lebombo lodge

The glass-walled suites of this elegant lodge seem to float

above the veld like an eagle on the wing.

The glass-walled suites are cantilevered against the hillside above the croc- and hippo-filled Nwanetsi River

PREVIOUS SPREAD At night, the pool area is given the romantic treatment with dozens of twinkling lanterns.

THIS SPREAD You can dine at the boma beneath beautiful candlelabra trees.

There are 21 suites at Singita Lebombo, each with views to the horizon and tranquil décor.

The suites merge smoothly with the vegetation.

A lion cub.

A petal-filled bath and a chilled bottle of bubbly await.

In the far eastern reaches of the Kruger National Park, near its border with Mozambique, there is a lodge whose drama and sheer magnificence of wildlife and flora are world-renowned. This is Singita Lebombo Lodge, tucked amongst ancient boulders on the slopes of the Lebombo Mountains in the 15 000-hectare Nwanetsi Concession Area. The lodge is one of two in the concession (the other is the simply stylish Sweni Lodge, a six-suited retreat of dark wood and elegant green furnishings, built in a wild setting on the Sweni River).

Having arrived from Johannesburg – a six-hour drive on easily negotiated national roads – we were led to our suite, one of 15 at Singita Lebombo. The glass-walled suites are cantilevered against the hillside above the croc- and hippo-filled Nwanetsi River and, once inside, there's a real sense of floating above the veld. At one end, softly draped curtains provided privacy for the bedroom. A king-sized bed, a small table and two chairs promised some quiet time ahead.

The living area was furnished with comfortable chairs, local baskets and a table bristling with books, magazines, games and playing cards. Boredom had no place here! I peeped into the bathroom, which held a couple-sized tub and fluffy towels. The colours were crisp white and earthy sand shades.

Returning to the main lodge, I looked back over my shoulder to the suites. Despite their glass walls and hi-tech interiors, they seemed to melt into the foliage and rocks. I was told that they were inspired by the nests of wild eagles that view the world from great heights.

This is Big Five country. Nwanetsi is on the migration routes of many animals, and sightings of lions, leopards and even the elusive African wild dog are common. And you're at liberty to explore the area in any way you fancy – you can requisition a private Land Rover, join game drives with other guests or take a guided bush walk.

There's also a spa, with three beauty therapists to pamper you with body treatments of your choice, from Thai massage, hot stone therapy and reflexology to spectacular outdoor mineral-salt scrubs and seaweed wraps.

I joined a game drive, and was rewarded with sightings of a mother lion and her cubs, and a group of lions hungrily devouring their kill. As the sun sank below the rose-tinted landscape, we returned to the lodge and its pebble-floored dining room for a delicious meal.

The culinary experience here is a highlight I'd never experienced before. On offer is a special 'tasting menu', consisting of small portions of all the dishes that are listed. Instead of having to select one or two dishes, guests can opt to compose their meal of a small helping of everything available. Meals can also be taken in the boma, surrounded by beautiful candelabra trees.

Replete, we wandered back along the lamplit path to our suite, accompanied by the sounds of the ubiquitous chirping crickets. There, the bath had been filled with bubbles and flower petals. Tea-light candles twinkled gently. Two hearts had been outlined in pebbles on the bathmat. A bottle of sparkling wine stood in an ice bucket.

Now that's what I call luxury.

details

When to go
Singita Lebombo Lodge is open all year round. Temperatures can be very high between November and February.

How to get there
Federal Air offers daily return flights from Oliver Tambo International in Johannesburg to Kruger National Park. Airlink and Nationwide fly daily to Kruger Mpumalanga International Airport near Nelspruit. If travelling by motor vehicle, the lodge lies 600 kilometres from Johannesburg, an easy six-hour drive on national roads.

Who to contact
Tel. (+27-21) 683 3424,
e-mail *singita@singita.com*
or go to *www.singita.com*

pafuri camp

The tented suites at Pafuri are linked by a meandering wooden walkway that overlooks the Luvuvhu River. Here you'll find untouched wilderness, wildlife galore, rare birds and links to ancient man.

I emerged onto my private deck to find a large dust cloud and a herd of thirsty buffaloes

PREVIOUS SPREAD The views from Lanner Gorge are wide, with the Luvuvhu River flowing silently far below.

THIS SPREAD Pafuri's thatched central lounge has seen many an entertaining evening, filled with stories of wildlife and the great outdoors.

The deck area at sunset – the perfect place to unwind after a day in the bush.

Twenty tented suites overlook the Luvuvhu River.

A drum summons guests to the dining room.

A buffalo will simply stand and stare if left alone; beware its temper when threatened, though.

I'd been on the road for most of the day when I arrived at Pafuri Camp in the remote northern reaches of the Kruger National Park. My first impression was of the giant jackalberry tree that grows through the deck of the lodge's main building, standing sentinel over the entrance. The second was of the silvery Luvuvhu River, which is the lifeblood of this vast wilderness.

Pafuri Camp stretches out in open-plan fashion on either side of its great-treed entrance, and all the buildings overlook the river. It is situated in a 24 000-hectare area called Pafuri or Makuleke, which is the ancestral home of the Makuleke people. This is known as one of the most diverse and scenically attractive areas in the Kruger National Park and, in 2007, the region was recognised as a wetland of international significance and was declared a Ramsar Site.

I was taken along a raised wooden walkway to my stilted tent. Some 20 tented suites line the river, each completely private and decorated in a simple, charming safari style. The wide, draped bed was inviting, the chairs were comfortable and the bathroom had a double basin and roomy shower. All around, huge windows overlooked the river and the bush.

Travel-weary, I decided to rest for a while, and was just nodding off when a huge bellow startled me into wakefulness. I emerged onto my private deck to find a large dust cloud and a herd of thirsty buffaloes. They rushed down to the sweet waters of the Luvuvhu River and jostled to get a drink. I decided to join them and watched from the shelter of my veranda, rock shandy in hand, and forgot all thoughts of sleep.

As the sun set rosily and the buffaloes, sated, were grazing peacefully on the bank opposite my tent, I heard a loud and frantic splashing. A huge crocodile had grabbed a buffalo calf and was dragging it beneath the water. The rest of the herd took off in alarm. A second crocodile joined the first, and I watched as the two reptiles twisted and tore at their victim.

I went to dinner, filled with my news. Later, around the fire, it was suggested that I visit Lanner Gorge, and I booked a trip. Leaving before sunrise, my guide and I scanned the area by spotlight to try to reveal any early-morning action. We drove along the river, and I was thrilled to see a pair of rare Pel's fishing-owls hunting on the banks. Further on, we encountered a pride of lions resting between hunting. The cats displayed some shyness to our presence, indicating the wildness of the area. Nearing the gorge, we met Johnson Mlambo, the camp's resident birding specialist. He was with a guest who had seen some 6 000 birds in her travels and had visited Pafuri to investigate its specials, and their binoculars were trained on a fruiting tree in which grey-headed parrots perched.

The sun had just broken the horizon when we reached Lanner Gorge, an ancient site with wonderful views across the Kruger. I stood on its precipitous edge. Some 150 metres below me, the Luvuvhu River flowed sluggishly, gently but irresistibly wearing away the rocky walls that lined its path. There's an abundance of evidence of humans occupying this area some two million years ago, and, in the more recent past, stone structures dating back 400 years indicate the existence of people whose ancestors have long left this land.

My appetite to learn more about this fascinating northerly part of the Kruger Park was whetted, as was my desire for breakfast, and I turned back to the lodge to start my investigation.

details

When to go
Pafuri Camp is open all year.

How to get there
Pafuri is a six-and-a-half-hour drive from Johannesburg, but the Punda Maria gate is the usual option for visitors coming from the south.

Who to contact
Tel. (+27-11) 257 5111,
e-mail *enquiry@safariadventure.co.za*
or go to *www.safariadventurecompany.com*

lowveld

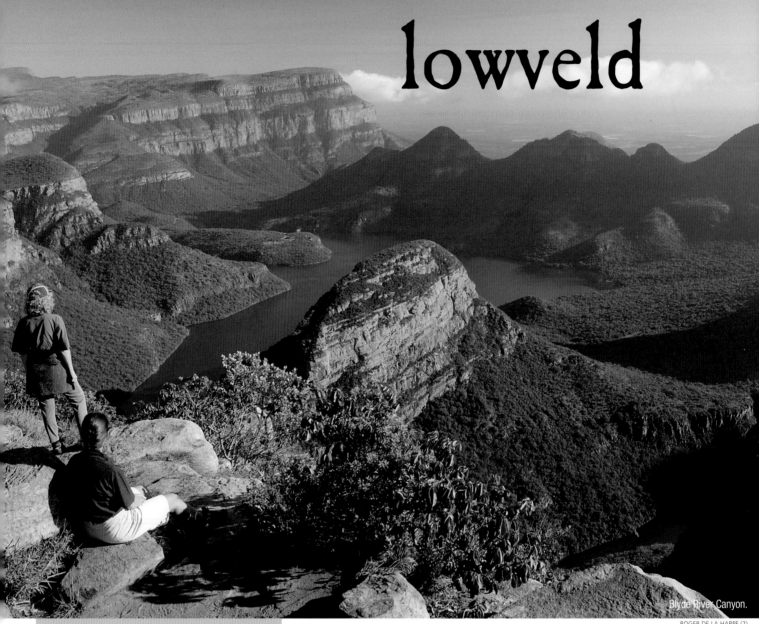

Blyde River Canyon.

ROGER DE LA HARPE (2)

THE HIGHLIGHT of the lowveld is the Kruger National Park, which can be reached by air easily from any of South Africa's major centres. Here, you'll have the ultimate bush adventure. Numerous private game lodges, most of which are serviced by their own airstrips, lie in concessions that offer a more intimate wildlife experience in open vehicles. To the west, the deep gash of the Blyde River Canyon and historical mining town of Pilgrim's Rest offer a day's distraction from the drama of close-up interaction with Africa's Big Five.

For itinerary suggestions, contact:
AFRICA GEOGRAPHIC TRAVEL
Tel. (+27-21) 762 2180
E-mail *travel@africageographic.com*
Website *www.africageographictravel.com*

Kruger & neighbouring reserves

South Africa's beloved Kruger National Park, and the wealth of luxury private reserves on its fringes, offer a wildlife experience that ranks with the best in Africa. At almost two million hectares, Kruger alone is home to an impressive number of species: 336 trees, 49 fish, 34 amphibians, 114 reptiles, 507 birds and 147 mammals. Conserved with the park's natural assets are historical and archaeological sites, from ancient rock paintings to 400-year-old stone constructions. Take a drive, visit the camps, which range from simple sites for tents to lodges for the well-heeled, and enjoy the magical scenery and game.

Blyde River Canyon

This deep gash in the earth's crust is the third-largest canyon in the world and one of South Africa's scenic wonders. The scenery of the 25 000-hectare reserve that surrounds it is unsurpassed, with varied and lush vegetation and a prolific birdlife, including the rare southern bald ibis. The canyon, which can be reached from Graskop via R532, runs from the moonscape rocky basins of Bourke's Luck Potholes and ends at the Three Rondavels. Stop at one of the many vantage points for a view of the 33-kilometre-long gorge.

Pilgrim's Rest

Once a booming 19th-century gold-mining town, Pilgrim's Rest was declared a living museum in the 1970s. Today, a museum is dedicated to the labours of the men who made and lost their fortunes here, and there are some extremely picturesque buildings.

White-water tubing on the Sabie River.

Chimpanzee Eden

The Jane Goodall Institute Chimpanzee Eden is set on a 1 000-hectare reserve some 15 kilometres from Nelspruit. Home to chimpanzees that have been misplaced from their natural habitat, the sanctuary is committed to the rescue and care of these apes.

Lowveld Botanical Garden

The 15-hectare Lowveld National Botanical Garden on the banks of the Crocodile River on the northern outskirts of Nelspruit is like an enormous arboretum, with its wealth of trees and evergreen lawns. Of the approximately 1 000 tree species that are indigenous to South Africa, over 650 can be seen in the garden, including baobabs, cabbage trees and wild figs, and a world-famous collection of rare cycads. More than 2 600 other plant species also occur.

Sudwala Caves

Step into the labyrinth that dives deep into the heart of the Mankelekele Mountain to discover mankind's oldest-known caves. The network was formed over three million years ago by trickling and seeping waters that slowly eroded the dolomite. A large area of the network has been mapped, but sections have never been seen by human eyes. Guided tours are offered throughout the day.

Guests with elephants at Camp Jabulani.

IAN JOHNSON

★ Pafuri Camp

○ Johannesburg

○ Durban

○ Cape Town ○ Port Elizabeth

MOZAMBIQUE

KRUGER NATIONAL PARK

LIMPOPO

Phalaborwa ○

Singita Lebombo Lodge ★

Camp Jabulani ★
Blyde River ●
Canyon   ★ Royal Malewane

                              Chitwa Chitwa
Ulusaba Private Game Reserve ★ ★ Game Lodge
Savanna Private Game Reserve ★ ★ Sabi Sabi Bush Lodge
Pilgrim's Rest ○   Sabi Sabi Earth Lodge ★ ★ Lion Sands Private
                                        ★ Game Reserve
Summerfields River   Tinga Private
Lodge & Rose Spa ★   Game Lodge

MPUMALANGA

● Sudwala Caves

Nelspruit ○

AFRICA
Geographic

An Africa Geographic publication
Africa Geographic
1st floor, Devonshire Court
20 Devonshire Road, Wynberg 7800
Cape Town, South Africa
www.africageographic.com

Reg. no. 1992/005883/07
First published 2008

Text & photographs © as credited individually, or as listed below:

Jeremy Jowell	*Winchester Mansions, Arniston Spa Hotel, RiverBend Lodge, Intsomi Forest Lodge, Oceana Beach & Wildlife Reserve, Mbotyi River Lodge, Lynton Hall, Leadwood Lodge, Rocktail Bay Lodge, Amakhosi Safari Lodge, Pakamisa, White Elephant Safari Lodge, Rovos Rail, Ant's Nest & Ant's Hill, Jembisa, Shibula Lodge*
Ian Johnson	*Jaci's Safari Lodge & Jaci's Tree Lodge, Mateya Lodge, Molori, Morukuru Lodge, Royal Madikwe, Tuningi Safari Lodge, Ulusaba Private Game Reserve, Camp Jabulani, Pafuri Camp*
Martin Harvey	*Summerfields River Lodge & Rose Spa, Lion Sands Private Game Reserve, Chitwa Chitwa Game Lodge, Sabi Sabi Earth Lodge & Sabi Sabi Bush Lodge, Savanna Private Game Reserve, Tinga Private Game Lodge, Royal Malewane, Singita Lebombo Lodge*
David Rogers	*Cape Grace, Steenberg Hotel, La Residence, Birkenhead House, Grootbos Private Nature Reserve*
Daryl Balfour	*Phantom Forest Eco Reserve, Camp Figtree, Samara Private Game Reserve, Mount Camdeboo Private Game Reserve*

Cover photographs © Ian Johnson

Editor Judy Beyer
Art Director Bryony Branch
Designer Cindy Armstrong
Project Manager Jenni Saunders
Travel coordinator Tracy Bennett

Reproduction in Cape Town by Resolution Colour (Pty) Ltd
Printed & bound by Tien Wah Press (Pte) Ltd, Singapore

ISBN 978 0 620 41172 1

AFRICA GEOGRAPHIC TRAVEL

Further information on all the establishments featured in *Safari in Style – South Africa* can be found at the end of each entry. Your local travel agent or consultant should also be able to provide help and advice. In addition, you are welcome to contact us at Africa Geographic Travel – we would be delighted to help you plan a visit to these properties or any other destination in Africa and its islands. Africa Geographic Travel offers many superb itineraries designed for the readers of *Africa Geographic* and *Africa – Birds & Birding* magazines. More about these can be found on our website.

Africa Geographic Travel
Devonshire Court
20 Devonshire Road
Wynberg 7800
Cape Town, South Africa
Tel. (+27-21) 762 2180
Fax (+27-21) 762 2246
E-mail *travel@africageographic.com*
Website *www.africageographictravel.com*